Arguments

Deductive
Logic
Exercises

Arguments

Deductive
Logic
Exercises_____ SECOND EDITION

Howard Pospesel
University of Miami

David Marans
Miami-Dade Community College

PRENTICE HALL, Englewood Cliffs, New Jersey 07632

Library of Congress Cataloging in Publication Data

POSPESEL, HOWARD (date)
    Arguments.

    1. Reasoning.   2. Logic—Problems, exercises,
etc.   I. Marans, David (date)   joint author.
II. Title.
BC177.P63 1978   162'.076   77-16006

Credits

© 1978 by Prentice-Hall, Inc.
A Simon & Schuster Company
Englewood Cliffs, New Jersey 07632

20 19 18 17 16 15

Printed in the United States of America

ISBN 0-13-045880-5

Prentice-Hall International (UK) Limited, *London*
Prentice-Hall of Australia Pty. Limited, *Sydney*
Prentice-Hall Canada Inc., *Toronto*
Prentice-Hall Hispanoamericana, S.A., *Mexico*
Prentice-Hall of India Private Limited, *New Delhi*
Prentice-Hall of Japan, Inc., *Tokyo*
Simon & Schuster Asia Pte. Ltd., *Singapore*
Editora Prentice-Hall do Brasil, Ltda., *Rio de Janeiro*

Contents

CHAPTER THREE
Property Logic

CHAPTER FOUR
Relational Logic

Preface
for Teachers_____

This collection of exercises is intended to be used as a companion for a logic textbook. Since the book uses no logic symbols and employs no specific logical techniques, it is compatible with any logic text. The need for *Arguments* stems from the fact that almost every logic book suffers from one or both of the following defects: an insufficient number of exercises and ones that are insignificant, contrived, and uninteresting. When a student encounters only exercises of the "If Alice marries Bob, Sue will be maid of honor" variety, he or she must wonder whether logic has any utility. We have tried to provide in this book nonartificial arguments with significant conclusions. More exercises have been included than would typically be used in a semester course so that fresh problems can be assigned in succeeding semesters. While this book is intended to supplement a text, its use would enable a teacher to substitute lectures for a textbook.

The exercises are divided into four chapters that correspond to commonly treated branches of logic. Within each chapter there are sentences to be symbolized and arguments to be evaluated. The final section in each chapter contains unformalized arguments quoted from actual sources. Work on these passages should help students identify and evaluate arguments encountered in their own reading. Sections 2.3, 3.2, and 4.2 contain only valid arguments and are designed for practice in constructing proofs. The exercises in sections 1.2, 1.3, 2.2, 3.3, and 4.3 include invalid, as well as valid, arguments and are intended for practicing other logical methods such as syllogistic rules, Venn diagrams, truth tables, and interpretations. Within each section exercises are ordered by difficulty. Very hard problems are marked "CHALLENGE."

In the second edition we have included for the first time 160 symbolization problems, and have replaced about half of the arguments in the first edition by better and more up-to-date examples.

Acknowledgments

Max Black reviewed the manuscript for the first edition. David H. Sanford, Hilary Freeman, David A. Spieler, and William de La Palme suggested improvements in the first edition that have been incorporated in the second. We are grateful to the University of Miami Philosophy Department for secretarial assistance and to Carmen and Michael Pospesel for help in proofreading.

The following friends contributed exercises: Steven Balas, Ray Bielec, Charlene Bollinger, Libby Cahill, Malcolm Campbell, Don Carignan, Ronald Cash, Lance Collaretti, David Cooper, Jerry Cranji, Raul Delgado, Edward Erwin, Becky Griffiths, Oron Hale, William Hanson, Bathsheva Kimmelman, Rachel Lerner, Elsa Martinez, Jorge Morales, Ellen-Sue Moss, Michael Nelligan, Denise Oehmig, Oliver Parker, Ernest Pons, Carmen Pospesel, Clara Pospesel, Jenny Pratt, James Rachels, Susan Reddy, Miguel Sanabria, Sheila Smith, Frank Vilasuso, Rocky Walters, Bill Whitman, Mark Woodhouse, and Harold Zellner.

Arguments

Deductive
Logic
Exercises

CHAPTER ONE

Syllogistic Logic

No greater misfortune could happen to anyone than that of developing a dislike for argument.

Plato

1·1 Categorical Propositions

Letters for abbreviating categorical terms are usually indicated by printing certain words entirely in capitals. The first letter of such a word abbreviates the term that contains the word. For example, the abbreviating letters for exercise one are N and W. Some exercises include a "dictionary" that specifies abbreviating letters.

1 "All NUDISTS WEAR clothing at meal time."

Miss Nude World

(W = persons who wear clothing at meal time)

2 "Some SCHOOLS are HELL-holes."

Critic Gilbert Highet

3 "Each APARTMENT has a VIEW of the ocean."

Advertisement

4 "No one in the White House STAFF was INVOLVED in this very bizarre incident."

Richard Nixon

5 "Every MAN is ENTITLED to his own opinion."

Sportswriter Elinor Kaine

6 "Some human ACTS are not DETERMINED."

Essay test

7 "Any person who makes OBSCENE phone calls needs professional HELP."

Joyce Brothers

8 "There are some who DISPUTE about Allah and SERVE rebellious devils."

The Koran

9 "None of the store EMPLOYEES was SHOT."

Newspaper

10 "Many CONTRARY-to-fact conditionals are not expressed in the SUBJUNCTIVE mood."

Philosopher Roderick Chisholm

11 "RUGBY players EAT their dead."

Bumper sticker

12 "There are no FOUR-legged GAY cats."

"Dear Abby"

(F = four-legged cats, G = gay creatures)

13 "Some PROSTITUTES are HOUSEWIVES who need extra money."

Newspaper

14 "A man who marries MONEY has to WORK for his living."

Bertrand Russell

15 "VULCANS never BLUFF."

Star Trek's Mr. Spock

16 "Individuals are occasionally born who belong to both sexes."

Pliny the Elder

(M = males, F = females)

17 "People who are intelligently INTERESTED in doing business and making money are not WARLIKE."

Harry Reasoner

18 "Many plants with MILKY sap are POISONOUS."

Tour guide

19 "He who HESITATES is LOST."

Proverb

20 "Plenty of people SEE the truth but cannot ATTAIN it."

Pascal

21 "MARIJUANA laws are unenforceable."

Editorial

(E = enforceable laws)

22 "The SCOTS are all MUSICIANS."

Eighteenth-century novel

23 "YOUR wife is a WITCH."

Sitcom dialogue

(Y = persons identical with your wife)

24 "Not all LAWS of nature are CAUSAL."

Philosophy text

25 "Spalding has made every baseball ever used in the major leagues." [1]

Newspaper

(S = Spalding baseballs, M = baseballs used in the major leagues)

[1] Now Rawlings makes all major league baseballs.

26 "There is an EVEN PRIME."

        Mathematics text

27 "WITH A NAME LIKE SMUCKER'S, IT HAS TO BE GOOD.®"

        Advertisement

(S = products named "Smucker's," G = products that have to be good)

28 "There's nothing that Miss Vicki DOES that ANNOYS me."

        Tiny Tim

29 "Where there is GAMBLING there is organized CRIME."

        Miami politician

30 "ALCOHOLICS are not all LIQUOR drinkers."

        Newspaper

31 "Only a MEDIOCRE person is always at his BEST."

        Laurence J. Peter

32 "ARTHUR was not a LARGE boy."

        Children's book

(A = persons identical with Arthur)

33 "Show me a SHOPLIFTER and I'll show you a THIEF."

        Public service advertisement

34 "It is untrue that all PROPOSITIONS can be EXPRESSED in subject-predicate form."   Philosopher J. P. Day

35 "None but a VIRTUOUS man is HAPPY."

        John Wesley

36 "He who WILLS to do evil in order to produce a greater good is a godless person."   Fichte

(G = believers in God)

37 "If they don't PLUMP when you cook 'em, they can't be
BALL Park franks."
                              Television advertisement

($P =$ wieners that plump when cooked)

38 "The only GOOD editor is a DEAD editor."
                              Reporter Hunter Thompson

39 "Every FRIGIDAIRE is not a REFRIGERATOR."
                              Advertisement

40 "I don't TAKE what I don't WANT."
                              Beatle lyrics

($T =$ things I take, $W =$ things I want)

Syllogism is of necessary use, even to the lovers of
truth, to show them the fallacies that are often
concealed in florid, witty or involved discourses.
                              John Locke

1·2 Syllogisms

41 Five Miami police cars responded to a complaint that a girl in
Coconut Grove Bayfront Park was indecently attired. One policeman
drove his cruiser onto the grass in spite of a sign reading "NO CARS OR
TRUCKS OF ANY KIND ALLOWED IN PARK." When a philosophy
graduate student complained to the policeman, the latter contended that
the sign did not apply to his cruiser. The student advanced the following
argument, but the policeman was unmoved:

No CARS are ALLOWED in the park. POLICE cruisers are
cars. Therefore, police cruisers are not allowed in the park.

Rocky Walters

42 Conversation between a four-year-old and her mother:

Amy: *"Mommy, what color are violets?"*

Mother: *"Purple."*

Amy: *"I saw some violets."*

Amy made this inference:

VIOLETS are PURPLE. Some of the flowers I SAW are purple. So, some of the flowers I saw are violets.

43 Any individual who has a definite set of rules of conduct by which he REGULATES his life would be a machine. No man has such a set of rules. Therefore, no men are machines.[2]

(R = individuals who have definite sets of rules of conduct by which they regulate their lives, A = machines, B = men)

44 The Indiana Senate recently approved a rather inclusive antipornography bill. Among other things, it prohibited "excretory functions" done publicly. But state Senator Lawrence Borst claimed the bill went too far.[3] Borst's concern is captured by 44.

All public acts of EXCRETION are PROHIBITED. Hence, public SWEATING is prohibited, given that a public act of sweating is a public act of excretion.

45 A master's thesis on the philosophy of mind contains the following passage:

Since the notion of being non-conscious is included in the very meaning of the word "machine," and since all robots are machines, it follows that no robots could be conscious.

The first premise may be rephrased 'No MACHINES are CONSCIOUS'. (R = robots)

46 Conclusive proof that the EARTH is spherical is provided by these two observations: (1) SPHERES cast CURVED shadows; and (2) the earth casts a curved shadow [on the moon during a lunar eclipse].

(E = planets identical to the earth)

47 News item:

Augusta, Maine—A bill in the state legislature reads: "Every person residing in Maine who earns less than $4,000 annually shall be furnished a hearing aid free of charge by the Department of Health and Welfare."

[2] This argument is discussed (but not advanced) by A. M. Turing in "Computing Machinery and Intelligence," *Mind*, LIX (1950), 452.
[3] "Sweating May Be Illegal," *Miami News*, January 28, 1974, p. 4-A.

Rep. Robert Soulas of Bangor said, "I guess this bill needs some work" when he was told his measure didn't say you had to be hard of hearing.[4]

The bill's defect is made explicit by the following syllogism:

Every person residing in MAINE who earns less than $4,000 annually shall be FURNISHED a hearing aid free of charge by the Department of Health and Welfare. Some Maine residents earning less than $4,000 per year are not HARD of hearing. Accordingly, some persons to whom the Department of Health and Welfare will supply free hearing aids are not hard of hearing.

(M = Maine residents earning less than $4,000 annually, F = persons who will be furnished free hearing aids by the Department of Health and Welfare)

48   Andy hopes the "little darlin'" will not draw this inference: [5]

ANDY WIPES his feet. But SINGLE blokes don't wipe their feet! Therefore, Andy must not be single.

(A = persons identical to Andy)

© Daily Mirror Newspapers Ltd. ANDY CAPP ® Dist. Field Newspaper Syndicate (May 11, 1974).

---

[4] "Maine Bill Needs to Be Polished Up" (Associated Press), *Miami News*, March 10, 1969, p. 6-A.

[5] See also exercise 361.

49 INVALID arguments do not ESTABLISH their conclusions. There are PROOFS of the existence of God that are not invalid. This shows that some proofs for God's existence establish their conclusions.

(I = invalid arguments)

50 No one who knowingly and needlessly ENDANGERS his or her health is RATIONAL. Thus, college students who SMOKE are not rational, because every college student who smokes is knowingly and unnecessarily endangering his or her health.

51 In April 1975, one of us gave an essay exam in Introduction to Philosophy on the freewill issue. Lectures preceding the test emphasized arguments and, not surprisingly, so did many of the exam papers. Exercises 51 through 53 (and 108) are exact quotations from these exams.

The soft determinist's argument runs as follows:
(1) All human acts are caused acts.
(2) A free act is always a caused act.
(3) So all human acts are free acts.

(H = human acts, C = caused acts, F = free acts)

52 From another exam:

Indeterminists believe that all human acts are caused, but some caused acts are not determined, therefore some human acts are not determined.

(H = human acts, C = caused acts, D = determined events)

53 From yet another paper:

An indeterminist might propose this argument:
(1) All human actions are events.
(2) Some events are free.
(3) So some human actions are free.

(H = human actions, E = events, F = free occurrences)

54 Many logicians propose 'implies' as a reading for the "horseshoe" statement connective. This is confused since 'implies' is a relational predicate, while the horseshoe symbol is a statement connective. As 54 attempts to prove, statement connectives are not relational predicates.

> Statement CONNECTIVES can be ITERATED (repeated); relational PREDICATES cannot.[6] Thus, statement connectives are not relational predicates.

55 A horoscope for Aries "reasons":

> *The moon causes the ebb and flow of the tide. The human body consists of about 70 percent water. Therefore, the moon influences our bodies.*[7]

The following syllogism is suggested:

> All the water on EARTH is influenced by the MOON. The water in our BODIES is water on earth. Therefore, the moon influences the water in our bodies.

(M = things influenced by the moon)

56 George O'Toole, writing in *Penthouse* on the assassination of John Kennedy, describes the Psychological Stress Evaluator as "a new type of lie detector that works through the medium of the voice." He tells what was discovered when tapes of Lee Harvey Oswald's postassassination interrogation were tested by this device.

> *His categorical denial that he shot anyone contains almost no stress at all. Stress is a necessary, but not sufficient, condition of lying. . . . The absence of stress is a sufficient condition of truthfulness. If someone is talking about a matter of real importance to himself and shows absolutely no stress, then he must be telling the truth.*
> *Oswald denied shooting anybody—the president, the policeman,*

---

[6] For example, S1 makes sense but S2 does not.

(S1) If Joe comes then if Sam comes Bob comes.
(S2) Joe killed Sam killed Bob.

For a discussion of this matter, see W. V. Quine, *Mathematical Logic*, rev. ed. (Cambridge, Mass.: Harvard University Press, 1958), pp. 23–33 (especially pp. 31–32).

[7] *Aries 1971 Horoscope* (New York: Simon & Schuster, Inc., 1970), p. 4.

anybody. The psychological stress evaluator said he was telling the truth.[8]

O'Toole's argument:

Spoken LIES exhibit STRESS. OSWALD'S denial did not show stress. Hence, the denial he uttered was not a lie.

(L = lying utterances, O = utterances identical to Oswald's denial)

57 When the Norfolk, Virginia, police department issued an order that off-duty officers carry personal handguns, it created a problem for its younger patrolmen.[9]

Some of the POLICEMEN who are required to carry personal handguns are not ALLOWED to purchase them, because (1) [according to Virginia law] nobody UNDER 21 is allowed to purchase a handgun, and (2) some of the police officers who must carry personal handguns are under 21.

(P = policemen who are required to carry personal handguns)

58 In *The Principles of Human Knowledge,* George Berkeley notes that the philosopher Locke reasons from the fact that brutes (that is, non-human animals) do not use words to the conclusion that they do not have the ability to form abstract general ideas.[10] Berkeley claims that the suppressed premise in this inference is 'the making use of words implies the having general ideas'. Is Berkeley right? Put another way, is 58 valid?

BRUTES do not use WORDS. All who use words have ABSTRACT general ideas. Hence, brutes do not have abstract general ideas.

59 Bertrand Russell writes:

The syllogism is only one kind of deductive argument. In mathematics, which is wholly deductive, syllogisms hardly ever occur.[11]

---

[8] April 1975, p. 126. Copyright 1975 by Penthouse International Ltd., and reprinted with the permission of the copyright owner.

[9] "New Cops Too Young for Guns" (Associated Press), *Miami News,* March 13, 1974, p. 15-A.

[10] (Indianapolis, Ind.: The Bobbs-Merrill Co., Inc., 1957), pp. 10–11.

[11] *A History of Western Philosophy* (New York: Simon & Schuster, Inc., 1945), p. 198.

He reasons syllogistically:

> Every argument in MATHEMATICS is DEDUCTIVE. Most
> mathematical arguments are not SYLLOGISTIC. This proves
> that some deductive arguments are not syllogisms.

60   A bit of dialogue from Joseph Heller's *Catch-22:*

> *You let them come in and look you over for a few minutes and I
> won't tell anyone you've been lying about your liver symptoms.*
>
> *Yossarian drew back from him farther. "You know about that?"*
>
> *"Of course I do. Give us some credit." The doctor chuckled amiably
> and lit another cigarette. "How do you expect anyone to believe
> you have a liver condition if you keep squeezing the nurses' tits
> every time you get a chance? You're going to have to give up sex if
> you want to convince people you've got an ailing liver."* [12]

The doctor's inference:

> No one with a LIVER condition is sexually ACTIVE.
> YOSSARIAN is sexually active. Consequently, he does not
> have a liver ailment.

(Y = persons identical to Yossarian)

61   Convicted Watergate conspirator Jeb Stuart Magruder on Richard
Nixon's role in the affair:

> *I know he was involved. Only a guilty person accepts a pardon.* [13]

Magruder reasons:

> Only a GUILTY person accepts a PARDON. Since NIXON
> accepted one, he must be guilty.

(N = persons identical to Nixon)

62   Is it possible to obtain knowledge in the empirical sciences? The
following syllogism aims to establish a negative answer to this question:

---

[12] Copyright © 1955, 1961 by Joseph Heller. Reprinted by permission of
Simon & Schuster, a Division of Gulf & Western Corporation.
[13] "Nixon Whitewash?" *Miami News,* May 4, 1977, p. 1-A.

A statement cannot be KNOWN if it could POSSIBLY be false.
It follows that no statement from the EMPIRICAL sciences can
be known, for any such statement could possibly be false.

(K = statements that can be known, P = statements whose falsity is a
possibility)

63 The preceding argument fails to establish its conclusion because its
first premise is false.[14] Argument 63 seeks to demonstrate the falsity of
that premise.

Some statements OUTSIDE the realm of logic and mathematics
can be KNOWN. Every statement outside this realm could
POSSIBLY be false. We conclude that some statements whose
falsity is a possibility can be known.

(O = statements outside the realm of logic and mathematics)

64 In defense of the first premise of 62, one could argue:

A statement cannot be KNOWN if it is FALSE. Any false
statement is a statement whose falsity is POSSIBLE. Therefore,
a statement cannot be known if it could possibly be false.

(K = statements that can be known)

65 News story:

*Canadian officials are refusing to comment on exactly how Mary
Steinhauser, 32, died yesterday when a prison siege ended in New
Westminster, B.C. The woman, a social worker, was shot twice,
but during the 41-hour siege officials said repeatedly that inmates
had only knives.*[15]

A syllogism underlies the story.

Whoever KILLED Mary Steinhauser had a GUN. The INMATES
had no guns. It follows that she was not killed by an inmate.

(K = killers of Mary Steinhauser)

---

[14] A person who subscribes to this premise is using unreasonably strict standards
for *knowledge.*

[15] "Who Killed Her?" *Miami News,* June 12, 1975, p. 8-A.

66 A newspaper feature discusses the content of this syllogism.[16]

Many MERCY-killers are treated LENIENTLY by the courts.
Thus, some PREMEDITATED murderers are given lenient
treatment by the courts, since mercy-killers are all
premeditated murderers.

67 Philosopher Jerome Shaffer writes:

*A mental event must happen to some particular person. Events
which happen to a body might have happened but not to that
particular person. So mental events cannot be events which happen
to a body.*[17]

(M = mental events, P = events that must happen to some particular
person, B = events that happen to a body)

68 Conclusive PROOFS are possible in every BRANCH of
mathematics. They are also possible in LOGIC. Logic, then,
must be a branch of mathematics.

(P = disciplines in which conclusive proofs are possible, L = disciplines
identical to logic)

69 At registration a student asked whether a philosophy course taken
"Credit Only" helps satisfy a minor in philosophy. Two rules were located in the college bulletin that bear on the question.

> (I) *Courses in which a grade of C or above must be recorded, may
> not be taken for "Credit Only."*

> (II) *A minor in philosophy consists of 12 credits passed with a grade
> of C or higher.*

This syllogism applies the rules to the case.

No "CREDIT Only" course will help satisfy a MINOR in
philosophy for the following reasons: only courses in which
a GRADE of *C* or higher is earned will help satisfy a philosophy

---

[16] "Few Mercy Killers Draw Full Penalties," *Miami News,* July 3, 1973, p. 3-A.
[17] Jerome Shaffer, "Persons and Their Bodies," *The Philosophical Review,*
LXXV (1966), 67.

minor, and no course in which a grade of *C* or above is made
is taken for "Credit Only."

(M = courses that help satisfy a philosophy minor)

70 In its strictest form the *verifiability criterion of meaning* attributes
empirical meaning only to those statements that are in principle conclusively verifiable.[18] Arguments 70 and 71 show that this strict criterion
has the embarrassing consequence that some scientific sentences lack
empirical meaning.

Only those statements that are in principle conclusively
VERIFIABLE are empirically MEANINGFUL. UNIVERSAL
statements are not conclusively verifiable even in principle.
Therefore, such statements lack empirical meaning.

71 UNIVERSAL statements lack empirical meaning. Many
scientific LAWS are universal statements. It follows that some
laws of science are not empirically MEANINGFUL.

72 The billboard suggests the following syllogism:

A really NICE home is HARD to find. Heather OAKS homes are
hard to find. Therefore, the homes at Heather Oaks are really
nice.

73 Some arguments with FALSE premises are VALID. This proves
that valid arguments do not always ESTABLISH their

[18] Arguments 223 and 224 also treat the verifiability criterion.

conclusions, because no argument that establishes its conclusion has false premises.

74 Philosopher A. J. Ayer writes:

There is no possible way of solving the problem of induction, as it is ordinarily conceived. And this means that it is a fictitious problem, since all genuine problems are at least theoretically capable of being solved.[19]

In this context 'fictitious' amounts to 'not genuine'. (S = solvable problems, I = problems identical to the problem of induction, G = genuine problems)

75 When Republican Senator John Tower asked Democratic Senator William Proxmire to contribute to Lenore Romney's campaign for one of the Senate seats from Michigan, he described her as "the rare and beautiful maiden whom the angels named Lenore." Proxmire replied to Tower's request:

I admire her charms. But I must question your view that beauty is a basis for a seat in the Senate, if for no other reason than the fact that neither you nor I could qualify.[20]

Proxmire's humorous reply seems to involve the following reasoning:

TOWER is a SENATOR. Tower is not BEAUTIFUL. So, beauty is not a sufficient condition for being a Senator.

(T = persons identical to Senator Tower)

76 Some philosophers of mind claim that any statement (or report) about mental phenomena is in actuality a statement about physical phenomena. Argument 76 attacks this view.

It is false that all MENTAL reports are PHYSICAL reports. For physical reports are always CORRIGIBLE (correctable), whereas some mental reports are not corrigible.

---

[19] *Language, Truth and Logic* (Harmondsworth, Middlesex: Penguin Books Ltd., 1971), p. 50.
[20] See "Quoth the Senator: 'Lenore? Nevermore. . . ,'" *Miami News*, September 23, 1970, p. 20-A.

77   From a college newspaper story:

> *There is no more hazing . . . allowed in branches of national fraternities. (All UM fraternities are branches of national clubs.)* [21]

Supply the missing conclusion. (H = *fraternities that permit hazing*, N = *branches of national fraternities*, M = *fraternities at UM*)

78   Any policy according to which the university acts as bail BONDSMAN for the student is an *in LOCO parentis* policy. Students FAVOR all such bail policies. Therefore, there is at least one *in loco parentis* policy that is favored by college students.

(B = policies that have the university making bail for its students, F = policies favored by students)

79   According to the philosopher J. L. Watling, Descartes held that any true proposition can be known on the basis of understanding alone.[22] Watling's criticism of this thesis is summarized by 79.

> Any proposition that can be KNOWN on the basis of understanding alone is LOGICALLY true. There are TRUE propositions that are not logically true. Thus, it is false that all true propositions can be known merely on the basis of understanding them.

(K = propositions that can be known on the basis of understanding alone)

80   News item:

> CHEYENNE, Wyo.—*The Wyoming Senate amended a proposed constitutional amendment yesterday, giving 19-year-olds the right to vote—if, in the case of men, they don't have long hair.*
>
> *The amendment, which didn't say anything about the length of women's hair, provided that haircuts of youths 19 and 20 must conform to military standards.*

---

[21] Herb Greenberg, "Fraternities Change Pledging Practices," *Miami Hurricane*, September 22, 1972, p. 3.

[22] "Descartes," in *A Critical History of Western Philosophy*, ed. D. J. O'Connor (New York: The Free Press, 1964), p. 172.

"When you accept the responsibility of a citizen, you should look like a citizen," said Senator J. W. Myers of Evanston.[23]

Myers appears to be "reasoning" as follows:

Young men with LONG hair do not look like CITIZENS. Only persons who look like citizens should be allowed to VOTE. So, no long-haired young men should be given the vote.

This argument is a collector's item. Only rarely does one encounter outside of logic texts an argument that is composed exclusively of absurd statements. (L = long-haired young men, C = persons who look like citizens)

81 The preceding argument could be attacked in several ways, including:

It is false that none of our founding FATHERS looked like CITIZENS. Some of our founding fathers were men who wore their hair LONG. Hence, it is false that no long-haired men look like citizens.

82 A magazine advertisement:

If you believe great bourbon has to taste heavy, you believe a myth. Because I. W. Harper is great bourbon that never tastes heavy.

This is a syllogism with the conclusion 'It is not true that all GREAT bourbons taste HEAVY'. (I = bourbons identical to I. W. Harper)

83 Philosopher Rudolf Carnap advances the following argument in *Meaning and Necessity:* [24]

A necessary condition for the ADEQUACY of any definition of 'L-true' is that it SATISFY convention 2–1. DEFINITION 2–2

[23] "Long Hair Would K.O. Vote Rights," *Miami News,* February 8, 1969, p. 1-A.
[24] (Chicago, Ill.: The University of Chicago Press, 1956), pp. 10–11.

satisfies convention 2–1. Hence, it is an adequate definition of 'L-true'.

(A = adequate definitions of 'L-true', S = definitions that satisfy convention 2–1, D = definitions identical to 2–2)

84 Robert Ardrey, writing in *African Genesis:*

> *Conclusions regarding animal behavior are valid only if confirmed by observations in the wild. Freud's generation knew nothing of the broader patterns of animal instinct, because science of that time confined its observations to captive animals.*[25]

Ardrey's argument:

> The conclusions about animal behavior drawn by the scientists of Freud's GENERATION were not confirmed by observations in the WILD. But conclusions regarding animal behavior are VALID only if they are confirmed by observations in the wild. Thus, no valid conclusions about the behavior of animals were drawn by the scientists of Freud's day.

85 Not all acts of CIVIL disobedience are VIOLENT. This fact shows that at least some acts of civil disobedience are MORALLY justified, since many nonviolent acts are justified from the moral standpoint.

86 The young woman's argument:

> The magic has GONE out of OUR relationship. Our relationship is not one of MARRIAGE. So, it is false that people have to be married for the magic to go out.

(G = relationships from which the magic has gone, O = relationships identical to ours, M = marriages)

---

[25] (New York: Dell Publishing Co., Inc., 1967), p. 21.

"I thought people had to be married for the magic to go out."

Drawing by Mahood; © 1972 The New
Yorker Magazine, Inc.

87   Joseph Epstein writes in *Harper's Magazine:*

> *Homosexuality has in fact formally had an outlaw status in this
> country for years, and laws against homosexuality, however
> unevenly enforced, are currently on the books of all but one of the
> United States. These laws are barbarous, not to say illogical:
> when committed by consenting adults, homosexuality is a crime
> without a victim, and for this reason alone the onus of criminality
> surely ought to be lifted.*[26]

Epstein's argument:

> The only acts that OUGHT to be regarded as criminal are those
> that involve a VICTIM. HOMOSEXUAL acts between
> consenting adults have no victims. Consequently, such actions
> ought not to be regarded as criminal.

[26] "Homo/Hetero: The Struggle for Sexual Identity" (September 1970), p. 50.

88   A newspaper editorial:

Little League baseball is supposed to introduce youngsters to the spirit of athletics, the desire to achieve, and the challenge of strong competition.

We note all of this because the Little League world series was held on the weekend at Williamsport, Pa., and the deal was rigged so that a U.S. team could finally win. How? Only U.S. boys teams were invited.

The sponsors had gotten tired of seeing children from Japan and Taiwan carry home the coveted league trophy (seven out of the last eight championships). So they simply barred the foreigners.

It was a pyrrhic victory for the Lakewood, N.J., youngsters who learned one more sports lesson: If you can't beat an opponent, don't try. Just get the adults to change the rules.[27]

This syllogism shows how the regulations guaranteed an American victory.

Only AMERICAN teams were INVITED. A team cannot WIN unless it is invited. It follows that the winning team has to be American.

(W = teams identical to the winning team)

89   In *A History of Western Philosophy*, Bertrand Russell writes:

All the important inferences outside logic and pure mathematics are inductive, not deductive; the only exceptions are law and theology, each of which derives its first principles from an unquestionable text, viz. the statute books or the scripture.[28]

One could attack Russell's thesis as follows:

At least some PHILOSOPHICAL arguments are important inferences that are OUTSIDE the areas of logic, mathematics, law, and theology. At least some inferences in philosophy are

[27] "Lesson for Kids," *Miami News*, August 26, 1975, p. 6-A.
[28] (New York: Simon & Schuster, Inc., 1945), p. 199.

not INDUCTIVE. Thus, it is false that all important inferences outside of logic, mathematics, law, and theology are inductive.

(O = important inferences outside of logic, mathematics, law, and theology)

90   (CHALLENGE) Saint Francis de Sales on the virtue of charity:

> *It is the business of charity to make us observe all God's commandments, generally and without exception. . . . Wherefore he who observes not all the commandments of God cannot be esteemed . . . good . . . ; since to be good he must be possessed of charity.*[29]

Regard the first sentence as expressing the claim that all charitable people observe all God's commandments. (C = people who possess charity, O = people who observe all God's commandments, G = good people)

> *Let my opponents prove that they were right, and refute me by argument, and I shall be greatly obliged to them.*
>
> Erasmus

1·3 Sorites

91   Columnist George Will writes:

> *[Justice Douglas] launches into a discussion of the inadequacy of standard aptitude tests as university admission criteria. And before he winds down he has made the inadequacy seem rather like unconstitutionality.*
>
> *He believes aptitude tests are invariably unfair because they inevitably reflect the "culture." . . .*
>
> *Douglas' key assumption is that racial groups often have their own separate cultures. . . . He is saying that where aptitude tests are*

---

[29] *Introduction to a Devout Life*, ed. Thomas Kepler (Cleveland, Ohio: The World Publishing Company, 1952), p. 27.

involved, cultural differences result in discrimination that is not distinguishable from racial discrimination. . . .

Because Douglas believes racial neutrality is a constitutional requirement, he must believe that the standard aptitude test is unconstitutional.[30]

According to Will, Justice Douglas reasoned:

Standard APTITUDE tests are culturally BIASED. Anything that is culturally biased is racially DISCRIMINATORY. Nothing that is discriminatory is CONSTITUTIONAL. Therefore, the standard aptitude test is unconstitutional.

92 J. S. Mill thought it possible to reason without generalizations, using only particulars. One of his arguments: [31]

Only LANGUAGE users employ GENERALIZATIONS. No ANIMALS have language. But some animals REASON. Hence, some reasoning beings do not employ generalizations.

93 The LAWS of physics are PROPOSITIONS. These physical laws will HOLD when all human minds have disappeared. Nothing that will hold when human minds have all disappeared is MIND-dependent. So, propositions are not mind-dependent.

(H = things that will hold when all human minds have disappeared)

94 The main character in Gilbert Millstein's *The Late Harvey Grossbeck* knows full well that science can plot the physical details of his life "down to the last dangling gangleon." Yet, affirming his uniqueness, Grossbeck proclaims:

I am infinite and they cannot embrace infinity. In the end, they cannot account for me.[32]

His argument:

GROSSBECK is an INFINITELY complex creature. Creatures of infinite complexity cannot be DESCRIBED in complete detail.

[30] "Selective Discrimination?" *Miami News,* May 10, 1974, p. 15-A.
[31] See J. P. Day, "John Stuart Mill," in *A Critical History of Western Philosophy,* ed. D. J. O'Connor (New York: The Free Press, 1964), p. 344.
[32] (Garden City, N.Y.: Doubleday & Company, Inc., 1974), p. 171.

Yet only that which can be so described can be totally
EXPLAINED. Hence, Grossbeck cannot be explained totally.

(G = persons identical to Grossbeck)

95 Logic students often express surprise when they are told that an
argument with logically contradictory premises must be valid. Argument
95 shows why this should be so. (It should be noted that even though
such arguments are valid, they do not establish their conclusions since
they have false premises.)

Any argument with a logically contradictory premise set has
premises that cannot possibly all be true. An argument whose
premises cannot possibly all be true is one that cannot
possibly have all true premises and a false conclusion. But all
arguments that cannot possibly have all true premises and a
false conclusion are VALID. Therefore, all arguments with
logically contradictory premises are valid.

(X = arguments having logically contradictory premise sets, Y = arguments whose premises cannot possibly all be true, Z = arguments that
cannot possibly have all true premises and a false conclusion)

96 The philosopher George Berkeley maintains that objects of ordinary
experience such as houses, mountains, and rivers do not exist when they
are not perceived. He supports this paradoxical contention with the
following reasoning: [33]

HOUSES do not exist UNPERCEIVED, for these reasons. A
house is something people PERCEIVE. We perceive only
IDEAS.[34] Ideas do not exist unperceived.

(U = things that exist unperceived)

97 When the director of campus security was asked to provide a campus
patrolman for a panel discussion of laws on and off the campus, he refused on the grounds that none of his policemen were qualified to speak

---

[33] *A Treatise Concerning the Principles of Human Knowledge* (Indianapolis,
Ind.: The Bobbs-Merrill Co., Inc., 1957), pp. 24–25. See exercise 331 for a related
Berkeleyan argument.
[34] The critical premise.

on campus regulations. He thereby opened himself to the following criticism:

> No person is qualified to SPEAK on the law unless he KNOWS the law. A person who does not know the law is not qualified to ENFORCE it. Thus, none of the campus POLICEMEN are qualified to enforce the law, since none are qualified to talk in public about the law.

98 Human ACTS are EVENTS. There are human acts for which humans are morally RESPONSIBLE. Any act for which a human is morally responsible is FREE. Free acts are not CAUSED events. So, the thesis [of determinism] that all events are caused is false.

99 In the early fifties a prospector named James Kidd vanished in Arizona, leaving a handwritten will directing that his fortune ($230,-000.00) "go into a research or some scientific proof of a soul of the human body which leaves at death." One hundred and thirty individuals and institutions filed for Kidd's estate, including Richard Spurney, a junior college teacher. Spurney submitted to the court a foot-thick pile of "evidence" that included three unpublished books. He had fifty "proofs" of the existence of the soul. Spurney summarized his main proof as follows:

> *Death is decomposition. Hence, what cannot decompose cannot die. But decomposition requires divisibility into parts. Thus what is not divisible into parts cannot die. But divisibility into parts requires matter. Hence what has no matter in it is not divisible into parts and so cannot decompose, and so is necessarily immortal.*[35]

This reasoning is paraphrased by 99. It is doubtful that all of the premises in this sorites are true, and Spurney presupposes just what he is supposed to prove (that a human soul exists). Nevertheless it is of interest to determine whether or not his argument is valid.

> Everything that DIES decomposes. Anything that decomposes divides into PARTS. Only MATERIAL things can be divided

---

[35] "Professor Claims Miner's Jackpot by 'Proving' Soul" (Associated Press), *Miami Herald*, March 27, 1967, p. 14-A.

into parts. The human SOUL is not material. Consequently, the human soul cannot die.

(A = things that decompose)

100 People sometimes regard false sentences as meaningless. In fact a sentence cannot be both false and meaningless. One might argue the point as follows:

Any sentence that says that something not the case is the case is FALSE. Any sentence that says that something not the case is the case is a sentence that maintains that something is the case. If a sentence asserts something to be the case, it cannot be MEANINGLESS. It follows that no sentence is both false and meaningless.

(Y = sentences that say that something not the case is the case, Z = sentences that say that something is the case, M = meaningless sentences)

Logic is the art of thinking well: the mind, like the body, requires to be trained before it can use its powers in the most advantageous way.
                                          Lord Kames

1·4 Natural Arguments

Each passage contains a syllogism or sorites. In some cases a premise or conclusion is unstated and must be supplied. Extraneous material should be ignored.

101 Prattle of a five-year-old:

"Monkeys like bananas, and I like bananas. So, I must be a monkey."

102 "Loaded questions aren't really arguments. Strictly speaking, then, they aren't fallacies, for only arguments can be fallacies."

Ronald Munson, *The Way of Words: An Informal Logic* (Boston, Mass.: Houghton Mifflin Company, 1976), p. 284.

103 "Any law that degrades human personality is unjust. All segregation statutes are unjust because segregation distorts the soul and damages the personality."

> Martin Luther King, Jr., "Letter from Birmingham City Jail," *The New Leader* (June 24, 1963), p. 6.

104

January 7, 1969, King Features Syndicate, Inc.

105 "Now they knew that she was a real princess, since she had felt the pea that was lying on the bedstead through twenty mattresses and twenty eiderdown quilts. Only a real princess could be so sensitive!"

> Hans Christian Andersen, "The Princess and the Pea," in *The Complete Fairy Tales and Stories* (Garden City, N.Y.: Doubleday & Company, Inc., 1974), p. 21.

106 "By Lemma b every [last line of a finished sequence] is λ-valid and by Lemma c a wff [well-formed formula] of the form Ψ & $\sim\Psi$ is not λ-valid. Hence no wff of the form Ψ & $\sim\Psi$ can be the last line of a finished sequence."

> John M. Anderson and Henry W. Johnstone, *Natural Deduction* (Belmont, Calif.: Wadsworth Publishing Company, 1965), p. 322.

107 "It is immediately obvious that not all necessary truths are known *a priori*; for there are necessary truths . . . that are not known at all, and *a fortiori* are not known *a priori*."

> Alvin Plantinga, *The Nature of Necessity* (Oxford: The Clarendon Press, 1974), p. 7.

108 "Indeterminism or the free will position states that some human acts are not determined. So, if some human acts are not determined, then some human acts are free (because no determined acts are free)."

From a midterm examination in Introduction to Philosophy, University of Miami, April 4, 1975.

109 "Every man who attacks my belief diminishes in some degree my confidence in it, and therefore makes me uneasy; and I am angry with him who makes me uneasy."

Samuel Johnson in James Boswell, *The Life of Samuel Johnson* (New York: Random House, Inc., n.d.), p. 618.

110 (CHALLENGE) "*Socrates.* And now, Laches, do you try and tell me in like manner, What is that common quality which is called courage . . . ?

"*Laches.* I should say that courage is a sort of endurance of the soul, if I am to speak of the universal nature which pervades [all cases of courage].

"*Soc.* But that is what we must do if we are to answer the question. And yet I cannot say that every kind of endurance is, in my opinion, to be deemed courage. Hear my reason: I am sure, Laches, that you would consider courage to be a very noble quality.

"*La.* Most noble, certainly.

"*Soc.* And you would say that a wise endurance is also good and noble?

"*La.* Very noble.

"*Soc.* But what would you say of a foolish endurance? Is not that, on the other hand, to be regarded as evil and hurtful?

"*La.* True.

"*Soc.* And is anything noble which is evil and hurtful?

"*La.* I ought not to say that, Socrates.

"*Soc.* Then you would not admit that sort of endurance to be courage—for it is not noble, but courage is noble?

"*La.* You are right."

Plato, "Laches," in *The Dialogues of Plato,* 2 vols., trans. B. Jowett (New York: Random House, 1892), I, 67–68.

CHAPTER TWO

Propositional Logic

> *We must not let it enter our minds that there may be no validity in argument.*
>
> Plato

2·1 Symbolization
Sentences

Letters for abbreviating simple statements are usually indicated by printing certain words entirely in capitals. The first letter of such a word abbreviates the statement that contains the word. For example, the abbreviating letter for exercise 111 is *C*. Some exercises include a "dictionary" that specifies abbreviating letters. Letters abbreviate affirmative statements. So, in exercise 111 *C* symbolizes 'I am a crook'.

111 "I am not a CROOK."

    Richard Nixon

112 "Either that man's a FRAUD or he's your BROTHER."

    Plautus

113 "If 14-year-olds had the VOTE, I'd be PRESIDENT."

    Evel Knievel

114 "A make-up TEST will be given if and only if you make ARRANGEMENTS with me prior to the scheduled date."

Course syllabus

115 "My husband has many fine QUALITIES, but he has one serious HANGUP."

Letter to "Dear Abby"

116 "Eight to ten thousand lives could be SAVED each year if people USED seat belts."

Insurance company advertisement

117 "It is untrue that Plato would ABOLISH all poets from his Republic."

Boccaccio

118 "War is CRUEL and you cannot REFINE it."

General William Sherman

119 "If Miami BEATS Cornell today and Penn State DEFEATS Michigan State Miami will WIN the tournament."

Newspaper

120 "Although kings CONFESS themselves to enjoy their thrones by the grace of God, yet they WISH to be adored in his stead."

John Calvin

121 "There is no Christmas in RUSSIA or Red CHINA."

Conservative slogan on Christmas tree price tag

122 "If God didn't WANT them sheared, He would not have MADE them sheep."

Eli Wallach in "The Magnificent Seven"

123 "Santa Claus is ALIVE and WELL and LIVING in Argentina."

Bumper sticker

124 "Possession of a HOT plate in the dorms is not illegal."

Student newspaper

(H = Possession of a hot plate in the dorms is legal)

125   "Should Senator Ervin RUN again, he would be a FORMIDABLE opponent."

Newspaper

126   "The club will raise ticket PRICES and/or get more television REVENUE."

Miami Dolphins owner Joe Robbie

127   "Neither CLARK nor ODOM was booked into the county jail."

Newspaper

128   "Florida faces the THREAT of power brownouts this summer unless the public CUTS back on its use of electricity."

Newspaper

129

"I've not only failed as a human being, I've failed as an international jewel thief!"

GRIN AND BEAR IT by George Lichty. ©
Field Enterprises, Inc., 1972. Courtesy of
Field Newspaper Syndicate.

(H = I have failed as a human being, J = I have failed as an international jewel thief)

130   "The university is making honest ATTEMPTS at integration only if it is actively RECRUITING a percentage of blacks

roughly equivalent to the percentage in the present U.S. population."

Letter to editor

131   "Ronald Reagan doesn't dye his HAIR, use MAKEUP, or DIET."

Newspaper

132   "If the Grand Jury calls me BACK I will be glad to COOPERATE fully if my IMMUNITY is extended."

CREEP operative

133   "I can either run the COUNTRY or control ALICE—not both."

Theodore Roosevelt

134   "You are sure to wind up PREGNANT if you don't STOP the intimacies and/or LEARN the facts."   "Dear Abby"

135   "Arthur could not PASS by the windmill without taking a RIDE on it."

Children's book

136   "If I FIGHT Ali and I LOSE, I won't be in the swimming POOL two hours afterwards—I will be in the HOSPITAL."

English boxer Richard Dunn

137   "[A man's] wearing an earring is neither immoral nor illegal."

"Dear Abby"

(M = A man's wearing an earring is moral, L = A man's wearing an earring is legal)

138   "If Congress does not FIND a way to force the banking industry to lower interest rates, and if the Securities and Exchange Commission does not STOP authorizing unjustified new financing by corporations, we will face an unbearable DEPRESSION."

Letter to editor

139 "Either the theories of scientific MEDICINE are right and those of the cultists are wrong, or the theories of the CULTISTS are right and those of scientific medicine are wrong."

AMA policy statement on chiropractic

140 "KISS me, and a handsome PRINCE will appear."

($K =$ You do kiss me)

THE WIZARD OF ID by permission of Johnny Hart and Field Enterprises, Inc. (February 25, 1971).

141 "Cook is a liar and a gentleman; Perry is neither."

Turn-of-the-century explorer

($A =$ Cook is a liar, $B =$ Cook is a gentleman, $C =$ Perry is a liar, $D =$ Perry is a gentleman)

142 "Provided, but only provided, that the French Fleet is SAILED forthwith for British harbors, His Majesty's Government give their full CONSENT to an armistice for France."

Churchill (June 1940)

143 "Nell will be a WOMAN soon, and she'll FORGET her brother unless he SHOWS himself sometimes."

Dickens, *The Old Curiosity Shop*

144 "Unless Thou wert incomprehensible Thou wouldst not be God."

Cardinal Newman

($C =$ Thou art comprehensible, $G =$ Thou art God)

145   "For the TENABILITY of the thesis that mathematics is logic it
is not only sufficient but also necessary that all mathematical
expressions be capable of DEFINITION on the basis solely
of logical ones."

Logician W. V. Quine

146

KERRY DRAKE by Alfred Andriola. © Field
Enterprises, Inc., 1972.

(K = I know what room they're headed for, W = Wiretapping is legal,
E = I have wiretapping equipment, P = I learn plenty in the next hour)

147   "Veracity is generally admirable, if not always prudent; but
credulity is neither admirable nor prudent."

Philosophers W. V. Quine
and Joseph Ullian

(A = Veracity is generally admirable, B = Veracity is always prudent,
C = Credulity is admirable, D = Credulity is prudent)

148   "The root causes of drug abuse can only be ATTACKED if the
federal government FOCUSES on the social forces behind it,
and if private citizens TAKE up most of the burden of
discouraging drug abuse."

Newspaper

149 (CHALLENGE) "Neither the Woodman nor the Scarecrow ever ate anything, but Dorothy was not made of TIN nor STRAW, and could not LIVE unless she was FED."

The Wizard of Oz

(W = The Woodman ate something sometimes, A = The scarecrow ate something sometimes)

150 (CHALLENGE) "If PETER gets on, Thor will go in as a RUNNER—unless he stretches it into a TRIPLE—in which case Thor will WARM up to relieve Clumsy if he doesn't have his STUFF."

B.C. by permission of Johnny Hart and Field Enterprises, Inc. (May 13, 1974).

It is not . . . the object of logic to determine whether conclusions be true or false; but whether what are asserted to be conclusions are conclusions."

Augustus De Morgan

2·2 Valid and Invalid Arguments

151 Flo's friend reasons:

Andy is POURING his own drink. If so, Flo can't be IN. Thus, Flo is not in.

152 In John 15:18–19, Jesus offers the following explanation of why the
world hates the Christian:

> *If you were of the world, the world would love its own; but
> because you are not of the world, [but I chose you out of the world,]
> therefore the world hates you.*

The conclusion may be paraphrased as 'The world does not love you'.
(W = You are of the world, L = The world loves you)

153 If Torricelli's hypothesis that the earth is surrounded by a sea
of air is CORRECT, then the length of the mercury column in
Perier's barometer DECREASED as he carried it up the
Puy-de-Dôme. The column did shorten [by about three inches]
as the barometer was carried up that mountain. It follows that
Torricelli's "sea of air" hypothesis is true.

154 Actor Cameron Mitchell's explanation of why he filed for bank-
ruptcy:

> *I had two choices—I could swallow a handful of sleeping pills, or I
> could declare myself bankrupt. My father was a minister, and he
> didn't believe in suicide. Neither do I. I chose bankruptcy.*[1]

A formalization of the argument:

> I am going to declare myself BANKRUPT, because it is either
> that or SUICIDE, and I will never kill myself.

[1] "Divorces and Parasites Leave Him Broke," *Miami News*, February 23, 1974,
p. 5-B.

155 If it RAINS for an hour a day for a week, the drought will be BROKEN. Thus, either it rains an hour each day for a week or the drought will not be broken.

156 News story:

Metro homicide detectives today expressed fear that two recent deaths were caused by a bad quality of heroin.

The deaths, police said, were caused by either extra potent doses or some unknown substance mixed with the drug.

. . . The two victims, police said, did not show the usual symptoms of heroin overdose. It was this, they said, that led them to believe that a poor quality of the drug or a bad mixture was now on the market.[2]

The detectives' reasoning:

The deaths were caused either by OVERDOSES of heroin or by BAD quality heroin. If the former, the victims would have shown the usual overdose SYMPTOMS. However, they did not exhibit these symptoms. Conclusion: the deaths were caused by bad quality heroin.

157 As the Celtics were winning the 1976 NBA Championship by beating the Phoenix Suns in Arizona, a television sportscaster claimed that the Celtics "are proving that they are a great basketball team, because you can't claim to be a great team if you can't win on the road." He was apparently reasoning as follows:

The Celtics can win AWAY games. They aren't a GREAT team if they can't win on the road. Hence, they are a great team.

158 Physiologist Knut Schmidt-Nielsen writing in *Scientific American:*

A crucial experiment was performed some 80 years ago by the French investigator J. M. Soum, who admitted carbon monoxide into the air sacs of birds in which he had blocked the connections to the rest of the respiratory system. If the air sacs had played any major role in gas exchange, the birds would of course have been

[2] Bill Gjebre, "Bad Heroin Feared in Deaths," *Miami News,* June 16, 1971, p. 5-A.

rapidly poisoned by the carbon monoxide. They remained completely unaffected. We can therefore conclude that the air sacs have no direct function in gas exchange.[3]

The last three sentences in this passage present an argument. (S = The air sacs play a major role in gas exchange, P = The birds are rapidly poisoned)

159 The old curmudgeon's argument:

If God hadn't WANTED there to be poor people, He would have MADE rich people more generous. Hence, He must want there to be poor people, since He did not make the rich more generous.

"If God hadn't wanted there to be poor people, He would have made us rich people more generous."

Drawing by Dana Fradon; © 1973 The New Yorker Magazine, Inc.

[3] "How Birds Breathe," *Scientific American* (December 1971), p. 75.

160 If theoretical terms are DEFINABLE by observational terms, then theoretical statements are TRANSLATABLE into observation statements. Consequently, if theoretical terms are not definable by observation terms, then theoretical statements cannot be translated into observation statements.

161 The woman speaking appears to have drawn the following inference:

Unless they HAVE a wok [by now], they don't WANT one as a present. If they do have a wok, they don't want one as a present. So, they do not want a wok for a present.

"The way I see it, if they don't already have a wok,
they probably don't want a wok."

Drawing by Modell; © 1973 The New
Yorker Magazine, Inc.

162 Russian mathematician Boris Kordemsky writes:

When two statements A and B are mutually exclusive, only one is true. Proving A *true by proving* B *false is called* proof by contradiction.[4]

Kordemsky seems to be describing this type of argument:

Statements *A* and *B* are not both true. Statement *B* is false. Therefore, *A* must be true.

(*C* = Statement *A* is true, *D* = Statement *B* is true)

163   A crisis arose when Carolyn King made the Orioles of Ypsilanti's American Little League. A newspaper article recounts the problem.

The national Little League has threatened to revoke Ypsilanti American's charter if Carolyn plays.

At first the league was ready to knuckle under. Then Ypsilanti city officials intervened and said Carolyn must be allowed to play or the American League wouldn't be allowed to use city ball fields.[5]

The local league's dilemma:

The national office will REVOKE our charter if Carolyn PLAYS. But either she plays or we will not be allowed to use the city ball FIELDS. So, either our charter is revoked or we cannot use the city ball fields.

164   A radio commercial states, "If you're thinking of orange juice but you're not thinking of *Orange Blossom*, then you're just not thinking of orange juice." The advertisers apparently think this entails the sentence 'If you're thinking of orange JUICE, then you're thinking of *Orange BLOSSOM*'. Does it?

165   Stopped at a traffic light, you notice that water is leaking onto the road from the car beside yours. You make the following inference:

Either their radiator is BOILING over or their AIR conditioner is on. Their WINDOWS are up even though the TEMPERATURE is 90 degrees. Thus, their radiator is not boiling over, because

[4] *The Moscow Puzzles* (New York: Charles Scribner's Sons, 1972), puzzle 276.
[5] "Little League Gets Its First Girl Player" (Associated Press), *Miami News*, May 11, 1973, p. 5-C. A year later, the national office dropped its "boys only" rule.

if the windows are closed while it is 90 outside, their air conditioner must be on.

166   Romans 14:8 is a very explicit argument.

If we live, we live to the Lord, and if we die, we die to the Lord; so then, whether we live or whether we die, we are the Lord's.

Here is a literal formalization.

If we LIVE we BELONG to the Lord, and if we DIE we belong to the Lord. Therefore, if we live or die we are the Lord's.

167   A. J. Ayer seems to advance the following argument in *Language, Truth and Logic:* [6]

If either SUBJECTIVISM or UTILITARIANISM is correct, then ethical concepts are REDUCIBLE to empirical concepts. However, neither of these ethical positions is correct. It follows that ethical concepts cannot be reduced to empirical concepts.

168   George Carlin appeared on television wearing a T-shirt that had this sentence printed on its front:

On the back of this shirt is a true statement.

The following sentence was displayed on the back:

On the front of this shirt is a false statement.

An argument that makes evident the contradiction:

The statement on the FRONT is true if and only if the one on the BACK is true. But the statement on the back is true if and only if the one on the front is not true. Hence, the statement on the front is, and is not, true.

169   It is common today for theologians to maintain that the Genesis creation story should not be viewed as literal description. But it is sur-

[6] (Harmondsworth, Middlesex: Penguin Books Ltd., 1971), pp. 138–40.

prising to find that the third-century church father Origen shared this position.[7] One of his arguments is paraphrased by 169.

> If the creation story is a true LITERAL description, then for the first THREE days of the earth's existence there was no sun. The concept of "day" is DEFINED by reference to the sun. It cannot be the case that both the concept is so defined and the earth existed three days before the sun was created. From this it follows that the creation story in Genesis is not true literal description.

(T = The earth existed three days before the sun was created)

170 In the sixth Meditation, Descartes argues: [8]

> BODY is by nature divisible. If so and if mind and body are one and the SAME, then MIND is also divisible. However, the mind is entirely indivisible. Consequently, mind and body are not the same.

171 The absent-minded coffee drinker reasons:

> Since my spoon is DRY I must not have sugared my coffee, because the spoon would be wet if I had stirred the coffee and I would not have stirred it unless I had put sugar in it.

(X = I sugared my coffee, Y = I stirred my coffee)

172 Some philosophers maintain that consciousness is a process in the brain. Argument 172 is a common criticism of this view.

> Consciousness cannot be a PROCESS in the brain without the sentence 'Jones feels a pain but nothing is happening inside his skull' being a LOGICAL contradiction. Now, that sentence is not a contradiction. Therefore, consciousness is not a process in the brain.

---

[7] See John Hick, *Philosophy of Religion* (Englewood Cliffs, N.J.: Prentice-Hall, Inc., 1963), p. 9.

[8] *Meditations on First Philosophy* (Indianapolis, Ind.: The Bobbs-Merrill Co., Inc., 1960), p. 81.

173 Philosopher U. T. Place believes the preceding argument to be mistaken. His criticism of it is paraphrased by this argument.[9]

> The first premise of 172 is TRUE only on the condition that the sentence 'Consciousness is a process in the brain' is a DEFINITION. However, that sentence is a scientific HYPOTHESIS, not a definition. The falsity of the first premise of 172 is sufficient to show that the argument is POOR. Hence, 172 is a poor argument.

174 The rules committee of the National Association of Basketball Coaches sponsored an experimental game using an 11-foot basket and a 30-second clock. Coach John Wooden, an advocate of the 30-second clock, commented:

> *Having the 11-foot basket and the 30-second clock tested in the same game won't tell you anything. They ought to try first the clock alone, then the 11-foot basket and see what the differences and the similarities are.*[10]

Perhaps coach Wooden was warning his colleagues about the following argument:

> If raising the BASKET to 11-feet is a good idea, and it is also a good idea to use a 30-second CLOCK, then the upcoming game will be SUCCESSFUL. Thus, if the game is not a success, neither the 11-foot basket nor the 30-second clock is a good idea.

175 A newspaper advertisement for a church includes these remarks:

> *If you don't believe the Bible is true—you are doomed. If you do believe it is true, but have not accepted its truth—you are doomed. So the choice is yours!* [11]

Do the first two sentences entail 'Either you ACCEPT the truth of the Bible or you are DOOMED'? (B = You believe the Bible is true)

---

[9] See U. T. Place, "Is Consciousness a Brain Process?" *British Journal of Psychology,* XLVII (1956), 44–50.
[10] "College Basketball Tries Two Changes" (Associated Press), *Miami Herald,* March 1, 1972, p. 2-F.
[11] *Miami News,* November 28, 1972, p. 5-B.

176 If intelligence is wholly HEREDITARY and provided that IDENTICAL twins have the same heredity, then being raised in separate households will not REDUCE the similarity of intelligence between two identical twins. But it does reduce the similarity. Identical twins come from a COMMON sperm and egg. If they do come from a common sperm and egg, then they have identical heredity. Therefore, intelligence is not entirely hereditary.[12]

177 Sportswriter Joe Gilmartin writes:

If Lanier really does come into his own, and if even one of the rookies comes through at forward, and if the club really hustles, it will finish third in the Midwest Division.

If none of the above happens, the club will still finish third in the Midwest Division.[13]

Does it follow that the club will finish third in the Midwest Division? (L = Lanier comes into his own, R = At least one rookie comes through at forward, H = The club hustles, T = The club finishes third in the Midwest Division)

178 A necessary condition that must be satisfied if our university is to become an OUTSTANDING school is the ADDITION of scholar-teachers to the faculty. The university will hire such people just in case tuition is RAISED. Consequently, raising tuition is a sufficient condition for our university to become an outstanding school.

179 In "The Pause of Mr. Clause" (from the album *Arlo*), Arlo Guthrie relates the frustration of an FBI agent who trails him to an airport where Arlo intends to fly "Youth Fare" on a plane with only one vacant seat.

The AGENT will fly only if GUTHRIE flies. Yet there is a SEAT for Guthrie if but only if the agent does not fly. And, obviously, Arlo will fly if and only if there is a seat available for him. So, Guthrie will fly and the agent will not.

---

[12] See H. H. Newman, F. N. Freeman, and K. J. Holzinger, *Twins: A Study of Heredity and Environment* (Chicago, Ill.: University of Chicago Press, 1937).

[13] *Street and Smith's Basketball Yearbook, 1972–73*, p. 102. Copyright © 1972 by The Condé Nast Publications Inc.

180 In the second chapter of II Kings, Elisha asks Elijah for a "double share" of his spirit. Elijah replies,

> *You have asked a hard thing; yet, if you see me as I am being taken from you, it shall be so for you; but if you do not see me, it shall not be so.*

Does Elijah's statement entail 'You will RECEIVE a double share of my spirit if and only if you SEE me as I am being taken from you'? ($A =$ You have asked a hard thing)

181 When I pick up the pizza should I leave the kids in the car?

> I cannot take both of them out of the car. But I will take MIKE and not AMY, only if I am WILLING to let Amy cry. Of course, I am not willing to let her cry. So, I will not take either child out of the car.

182 JOE is fat. So, either SALLY is ugly or she is not ugly.

183 The preceding argument is a peculiar and apparently worthless argument. Why, then, should it have tested out as it did? This argument offers an explanation.

> Argument 182 is VALID, for the following reasons. It is valid if and only if it is logically impossible for its premise to be true while its conclusion is false. It is logically impossible for its conclusion to be false; and if this is so, then it is logically impossible for its premise to be true while its conclusion is false.

($A =$ It is logically possible for the premise of 182 to be true while its conclusion is false, $B =$ It is logically possible for the conclusion of 182 to be false)

184 Part of a poem by R. D. Laing:

> *I am stupid every way:*
> *to think I'm stupid, if I am stupid*
> *to think I'm stupid if I'm not stupid.*[14]

---

[14] R. D. Laing, *Knots* (New York: Random House, 1970), p. 22. Reprinted by permission of Pantheon Books, a division of Random House, Inc.

The passage suggests an argument.

> If I am STUPID and THINK I'm stupid, then I am stupid.
> If I'm not stupid but think I am, then I am stupid. It
> follows that my thinking I am stupid is a sufficient condition
> of my being stupid.

185 A newspaper story:

> *Sen. William Scott (R-Va.) denied yesterday that he was "the*
> *dumbest" member of Congress, as* New Times *magazine said he*
> *was, but, he added, he was in a quandary whether it would be wise*
> *to take the matter to court.*
>
> *. . . He hasn't decided yet whether to file a libel suit against* New
> Times, *Scott said, because in libel suits the element of malice, a*
> *crucial point, is very hard to prove.*
>
> *"I don't want to bring a suit that I don't win, because somebody*
> *might think the article is true if I don't win," he said.*[15]

Senator Scott is afraid some people would reason:

> Scott WINS the case if and only if the article is both false and
> MALICIOUS. Therefore, if Scott does not win the case, the
> article must be TRUE.

186 How ought sentences of the form 'Only A are B' be put into
standard form? For example, should S1 be translated as S2 or S3?

> (S1) Only intelligent persons are physicists.
> (S2) All intelligent persons are physicists.
> (S3) All physicists are intelligent persons.

Argument 186 attempts to answer this question.

> S1 translates into standard form as S3, and not as S2. The proof:
> S1 translates into standard form either as S2 or as S3 but not
> both. If the former, then the truth of S1 is both a necessary
> and a sufficient condition for the truth of S2. But S1 is true,
> while S2 is false.

[15] "Sen. Scott Won't Test His Intelligence," *Miami News*, May 24, 1974, p. 7-C.

($A =$ S1 translates into standard form as S3, $B =$ S1 translates into standard form as S2, $C =$ S1 is true, $D =$ S2 is true)

187 (CHALLENGE) Logicians G. E. Hughes and M. J. Cresswell write,

> *This proposition will be true iff [if and only if] at least one of the original propositions is true, and therefore false iff both of these are false.*[16]

($T =$ This proposition is true, $F =$ The first of the original propositions is true, $S =$ The second of the original propositions is true)

188 (CHALLENGE) Elsewhere in the same book Hughes and Cresswell say:

> *Sometimes a formula containing occurrences of $\supset$ is a thesis, but when $\supset$ is replaced by $\ni$ the formula ceases to be a thesis. (Of course this will never be the case when the only occurrence of $\supset$ so replaced is the main operator, for then either both formulae are theses or neither is.)*[17]

The sentence in parentheses expresses an argument.

> If the only horseshoe replaced is the MAIN operator, then either both formulas are theses or neither is. Thus, if the only horseshoe replaced is the main operator it is false that both the FIRST formula is and the SECOND formula is not a thesis.

189 (CHALLENGE)

> If any one of the three positions of HARD determinism, SOFT determinism, and INDETERMINISM is correct, then the other two are mistaken.[18] So, one of these three positions is correct, and the other two are incorrect.

[16] *An Introduction to Modal Logic* (London: Methuen and Co. Ltd., 1968), p. 5.

[17] Ibid., p. 38.

[18] For an explanation of these three terms see William James's essay "The Dilemma of Determinism" in *Essays in Pragmatism,* ed. Alburey Castell (New York: Hafner Publishing Co., Inc., 1948). See especially pp. 40–41.

190 (CHALLENGE) Pascal's famous wager is paraphrased by 190.[19]

If I BELIEVE in God, then (1) if he EXISTS I GAIN, and (2) if he does not then (at least) I do not LOSE. If, on the other hand, I do not believe, then (1) if God exists I lose, and (2) if he does not I do not gain. From this it follows that if I believe I will either gain or (at least) not lose, while if I do not believe I will either lose or (at best) fail to gain.

Grammar is the logic of speech, even as logic is the grammar of reason.

R. C. Trench

2·3 Valid Arguments

191 An Associated Press story:

CONCORD, N.C.—A married woman in her late 20s says she has been going topless for the last four years when the weather is pleasant, when she is working in her yard, driving her car or riding a motorcycle with her husband.

. . . A state highway patrolman, T. L. Hooks, stopped her Sunday while she was riding topless on a motorcycle with her husband.

. . . Hooks said he later let her go because there is no law prohibiting her from being topless in public. "I guess it's not legally indecent to do that," he said, "but I still believe it's improper. It could cause accidents."

The woman's husband supports her action. "You can't have two sets of moral values, one for men and the other for women," he said.

And she says: "If a man can go without a shirt, then so can I. There's not much difference between the chest of a man and the chest of a woman. A little more fat on the woman, a little more hair on the man. . . ." [20]

[19] See his *Pensées*, number 233.
[20] " 'If a Man Can Go Without a Shirt, Then So Can I' " (Associated Press), *Miami News*, July 25, 1974, p. 1-A.

The couple's argument seems to be simply:

> If MEN are allowed to be shirtless in public, then so should WOMEN. Of course, men are allowed to go without a shirt in public. Hence, women should be permitted to appear shirtless in public.

192   Historian of science A. C. Crombie states,

> *Some later Greek writers had used erosion by water as evidence for the temporal origin of the earth, for, they argued, if the earth had existed from eternity all mountains and other features would by now have disappeared.*[21]

The Greeks reasoned:

> The mountains have not DISAPPEARED. If the earth had existed from ETERNITY, the mountains would by now have disappeared. It follows that the earth is not eternal.

193   Dolphin guard Bob Kuechenberg gives this account of how he decided to attend college:

> *"My father and uncle were human cannonballs in carnivals,"* Kuechenberg says. *"My father told me, go to college or be a cannonball. Then one day my uncle came out of the cannon, missed the net and hit the Ferris wheel. I decided to go to school."* [22]

Not only can Kuechenberg play football, he draws a mean inference.

> I will either go to SCHOOL or be a CANNONBALL. But I will not become a cannonball. Therefore, I will go to school.

194   Uncle Phil's 'OMIGOSH!' indicates that he has just drawn the following inference:

> Dr. Tufts was not both in MIAMI and in SWITZERLAND. Since he was in Switzerland, he was not in Miami.

[21] *Medieval and Early Modern Science* (Garden City, N.Y.: Doubleday & Company, Inc., 1959), I, 123.
[22] " 'Who *Are* Those Guys?' " *Newsweek*, January 17, 1972, p. 52.

Reprinted with permission of the Mc-
Naught Syndicate, Inc.

195   Newspaper story:

*An interesting switch was pulled in Rome yesterday by Adam
Nordwall, an American Chippewa Indian chief. As he descended
from his plane from California dressed in full tribal regalia
Nordwall announced in the name of the American Indian people
that he was taking possession of Italy "by right of discovery" in
the same way Christopher Columbus did in America.*

*"I proclaim this day the day of the discovery of Italy," said
Nordwall, who teaches at California State University. "What right
did Columbus have to discover America when it had already been
inhabited for thousands of years? The same right that I have to
come now to Italy and proclaim the discovery of your country."* [23]

The Chippewa chief invites us to reason:

COLUMBUS discovered America if and only if NORDWALL
discovered Italy. Hence, Columbus did not discover America,
since Nordwall clearly did not discover Italy.

196   Marylou's argument:

If there were SOMEONE else, my mother would not be
CARRYING on so. Since she is carrying on it follows that there
is no one else.

[23] "Chief Challenges Columbus Right," *Miami News,* September 25, 1973,
p. 2-A.

MOMMA by Mell Lazarus. Courtesy of Mell Lazarus and Field Newspaper Syndicate (February 15, 1975).

197 Medieval scholars denied the possibility of a complete vacuum. One of their reasons is founded on a medieval belief about motion.[24]

> The SPEED of an object varies in inverse proportion to the resistance provided by the medium in which the object is moving. Assuming this is so, then if there exists a perfect VACUUM some bodies move with INFINITE speed. However, no body could move with infinite speed. Consequently, there is no perfect vacuum.

198 Logician Geoffrey Hunter discussing a formal system of arithmetic, S:

> *If S is decidable then S is not respectable. So if S is respectable S is undecidable.*[25]

'Decidable' and 'respectable' as used here are technical terms. ($D = S$ is decidable, $R = S$ is respectable)

199 The following argument provides an explanation for the rapidly rising costs of college education:

> LABOR costs are rising in all sectors of the economy. In most areas these costs are OFFSET by increased worker productivity [as a result of automation]. Increased labor costs

[24] See Herbert Butterfield, *The Origins of Modern Science* (New York: The Free Press, 1957), p. 16.

[25] *Metalogic* (Berkeley and Los Angeles, Calif.: University of California Press, 1971), p. 225.

in the field of higher EDUCATION [faculty raises] are not offset by increased productivity [number of students taught]. If all of the preceding is true, then the COST of college education is increasing at a rate that is well above the general cost of living. We can conclude that the cost of higher education is increasing at a rate well above the general cost of living.

200   Using a telescope, Galileo was able to observe all the phases of the planet Venus. Physics professor Verne Booth explains what that must have meant to Galileo.

> *This was a triumph of the greatest importance for the Copernicans, for in the Ptolemaic system, Venus could never get far enough away from the sun to show a full phase. The fact that Venus displays a full set of phases constitutes the one conclusive proof that it revolves around the sun.*[26]

The argument that underlies this passage:

Either the COPERNICAN or the PTOLEMAIC theory is true. If the latter is true, Venus cannot show a FULL phase. It follows that the Copernican theory is true, for Venus does display a full phase.

201   Sally reasons:

If there were no school BOARD I would not have GONE to school, and if I had not gone to school I would not have LOST my mitten. Therefore, if there were no school board I would not have lost the mitten.

© 1970 United Feature Syndicate, Inc.

[26] Verne H. Booth, *Physical Science* (New York: The Macmillan Company, 1967), p. 57.

202   A fishing columnist writes:

The fishing was slow because there was no wind. That meant the water was too clear, and the fish aren't going to be biting in clear waters.[27]

This explanation is an argument.

The fish were not BITING because there was no WIND. If there is no wind the water is CLEAR, and fish will not bite if the water is clear.

203   Eb reasons:

The sweater will be too BIG or too SMALL. If it's too big she'll be FLATTERED, and if it's too small she'll WEAR it! So, either she'll be flattered or she'll wear the sweater.

© 1973 United Feature Syndicate, Inc.

204   If Cain married his SISTER, their marriage was INCESTUOUS. If he did not marry his sister, then Adam and Eve were not the PROGENITORS of the entire human race. It follows that Adam and Eve were the progenitors of the whole human race only if Cain's marriage was incestuous.

205   A humanities test contains the following multiple-choice question:

Plato was:
(a) the teacher of Socrates;
(b) the teacher of Aristotle;

[27] Jeff Klinkenberg, "He Tells It Like It Is—and That Isn't Good," *Miami News,* May 8, 1974, p. 2-D.

(c) the teacher of Plotinus;
(d) all of the above;
(e) none of the above.

A thinking student who knows that Plato taught Aristotle but did not teach Socrates can be sure of answering the question correctly even if he or she has never heard of Plotinus. The student reasons:

> Plato taught ARISTOTLE. If this is so, then the correct answer is either *b* or *d*. The correct answer is *d* only if Plato taught SOCRATES. Since Plato was not Socrates's teacher, the correct answer has to be *b*.

(B = The correct answer is b, D = The correct answer is d)

206 "Curious Daughter" writes:

DEAR ABBY:

I am 30 years old and reasonably well adjusted although I grew up without a father.

My mother told me that a few months after she married my father, he was killed in the war. It didn't take too much intelligence to figure out that if my father had really been killed in the war he would have been considered a hero in the eyes of his widow, and she'd have kept his memory alive with pictures, letters and souvenirs to be shared with his family. . . .

I have concluded that I am illegitimate.[28]

Curious advances this argument:

> If my father had really been KILLED in the war, he would have been a HERO. Had he been a hero his memory would be kept ALIVE. But his memory was allowed to die. If my father was not killed in the war, my mother has been LYING to me about him. She would lie about him only if I am ILLEGITIMATE. I have concluded that I am illegitimate.

[28] Abigail Van Buren, "Dear Abby" (Chicago Tribune–New York News Syndicate, Inc.), *Miami News*, April 10, 1973, p. 6-C. Reprinted by permission.

207   Conversation overheard on campus:

First student: "Did you go to Spanish yesterday?"

Second student: "Did you? Oh, you wouldn't be asking me."

The second student may have reasoned:

He cannot both have GONE to class and now be ASKING if I went to class. Hence, if he asks whether I went to class, he did not go.

208   Set theory is incomplete, if it is consistent.[29] Consequently, it is false that set theory is both consistent and complete.

($A =$ Set theory is complete, $B =$ Set theory is consistent)

209   Prove that the wife's comments entail 'The martini is either for CELEBRATING or to cheer you UP'. ($R =$ You got the raise)

"IF YOU GOT THE RAISE, IT'S TO CELEBRATE. IF YOU DIDN'T, IT'S TO CHEER YOU UP!"

210   The score stands at Miami 16–Penn State 21, as a result of a Miami touchdown. Now the Miami coach must decide whether to send in a one-

---

[29] The premise of this argument was proved by Austrian-American logician Kurt Gödel.

point or a two-point play. His reasoning (which, of course, takes place in a flash) may be represented as follows:

> Seventeen points plus a touchdown will put us ahead, but so will 16 points plus a touchdown. On the other hand, 17 points plus a field goal will still leave us behind. If all of this is so, then there is no advantage in scoring just one point. Eighteen points plus a field goal will give us a tie. If 18 points and a field goal would produce a tie, then there is something to be gained by attempting the two-point conversion. Therefore, there is no advantage in scoring one point, but there is something to be gained by trying a two-point play.

Use these symbols:

> A = 17 points plus a touchdown will put us ahead
> B = 16 points plus a touchdown will put us ahead
> C = 17 points plus a field goal will leave us behind
> D = There is an advantage in scoring one point
> E = 18 points plus a field goal will give us a tie
> F = There is something to be gained by attempting the two-point conversion

211   From a gossip column:

> Q: *Isn't there a scandalous story about Rhodesian strongman Ian Smith that's being hushed up?—Verone P., Richmond, Va.*
>
> A: *It's not the Prime Minister who's in trouble. It's his 22-year-old son Alex. Caught with a pound of marijuana in the car while crossing the Rhodesian-Mozambique border with four male friends and a girl. Rhodesia's attorney general is faced with a difficult decision—to prosecute the son and risk embarrassing Prime Minister Smith, or to drop charges and risk a mess with the press.*[30]

The attorney general's dilemma:

> Either I EMBARRASS the Prime Minister or I get ATTACKED by the press. For if I PROSECUTE, I will embarrass the Prime Minister; and if I DROP the charges, the press will attack me. Yet I must do one of the two—either prosecute or drop the charges.

[30] GLAD YOU ASKED THAT by Marilyn and Hy Gardner. Courtesy of Field Newspaper Syndicate. (February 29, 1972)

212   Where in the body is hunger detected? The three classic answers are (1) the stomach, (2) cells throughout the body, and (3) the brain.[31] Arguments 212 through 214 defend these views. The following argument summarizes the reasoning of A. J. Carlson: [32]

> WHENEVER the empty stomach shows strong contractions, the subject invariably signals that he feels hunger. If so, then the STOMACH is the basic source of hunger unless the central nervous system CONTROLS these contractions. A hungry DOG whose stomach neural connections have been severed experiences stomach contractions. This observation is incompatible with the thesis that stomach contractions are controlled by the central nervous system. Thus, we have shown the stomach itself to be the basic source of hunger.

213   The French psychologist Joanny Roux reasoned in an 1897 paper: [33]

> Hunger is caused either by the STOMACH or by the blood acting on the BRAIN or by ALL the cells of the body. If the stomach causes hunger, then the REMOVAL of all the nerves connected to a rabbit's stomach will prevent normal eating. But doing this to a rabbit does not prevent normal eating. Cerebral activity always starts with stimulation at the PERIPHERY. If so, then hunger is not caused by the blood acting on the brain. It follows that hunger must be caused by all the cells of the body.

214   A number of contemporary scientists have contributed to the following reasoning: [34]

> The BRAIN is the cause of hunger, and the specific MECHANISM is the detection of the difference of glucose levels between arteries and veins. Proof: After one region of an animal's hypothalamus has been destroyed, the animal becomes OBESE. When a different region in the hypothalamus has been destroyed, the animal CEASES to eat. ELECTRICAL

---

[31] For a detailed history of this problem see Mark R. Rosenzweig, "The Mechanisms of Hunger and Thirst," in *Psychology in the Making*, ed. Leo Postman (New York: Alfred A. Knopf, Inc., 1962).

[32] *The Control of Hunger in Health and Disease.*

[33] "La Faim, Étude Physio-psychologique," *Bulletin de la Société d'Anthropologie de Lyon*, XVI (1897), 409–55. His view is explained in Rosenzweig, "The Mechanisms of Hunger and Thirst," pp. 96–97.

[34] See Rosenzweig, pp. 115–23.

stimulation of the hypothalamus can cause both eating and the cessation of eating. All of these facts taken together mean that the brain is the cause of hunger. If the brain is the cause, then if GLUCOSE is the primary cell food the specific mechanism must be the detection of difference between arterial and venous glucose levels. Glucose is the main cell food.

215 In his essay "An Apology for Raimond Sebond," the skeptic Montaigne argues that humans are not superior to other animals even in ability to reason. In support he offers this story:

> *Chrysippus, albeit in other things as disdainfull a judge of the condition of beasts as any other Philosopher, considering the earnest movings of the dog, who comming into a path that led three severall wayes in search or quest of his Master, whom he had lost, or in pursuit of some prey that hath escaped him, goeth senting first one way and then another, and having assured himself of two, because he findeth not the tracke of what he hunteth for, without more adoe furiously betakes himselfe to the third; he is enforced to confesse that such a dog must necessarily discourse thus with himselfe, "I have followed my Masters footing hitherto, hee must of necessity pass by one of these three wayes; it is neither this nor that, then consequently hee is gone this other." And by this conclusion of discourse assuring himselfe, comming to the third path, hee useth his sense no more, nor sounds it any longer, but by the power of reason suffers himselfe violently to be carried through it.*[35]

Formalize the dog's argument and show that it is valid. (F = My master walked the first path, S = My master walked the second path, T = My master walked the third path)

216 The *Braheian Debater* is a newspaper devoted to defending the view that the earth is the fixed center of the universe. One issue prints the following excerpt from a critical letter:

> *If every satellite must move to remain in orbit, and if earth does not move, then there cannot be what is called a "geosynchronous" satellite. [A geosynchronous satellite appears to be motionless in the sky and appears to remain directly above a certain fixed point on the earth.]*

[35] Michel de Montaigne, *Essayes*, IV (London: Gibbings & Co., 1603), 331–32.

But geosynchronous satellites exist. [Many communications and some weather satellites are geosynchronous.]

[But geosynchronous satellites are impossible in a theory of a motionless earth.] Therefore, the earth must move! [36]

Supply this unstated premise: 'Every SATELLITE must move to remain in orbit'. Do not symbolize the bracketed material. (E = The earth moves, G = Geosynchronous satellites exist)

217 The "B. C." strip suggests this argument:

Dick and Jane can take a TRIP only if they place their pets in a KENNEL. If they put their pets in a kennel they will SPEND all their money. But if they spend all their money they cannot take a trip. So, Dick and Jane cannot take a trip.

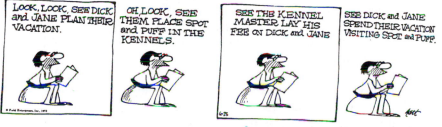

B.C. by permission of Johnny Hart and Field Enterprises, Inc. (June 25, 1973).

218 Ninety-six percent of those persons who have a manic-depressive identical TWIN are themselves manic-depressive, while only 23 percent of those persons who have a manic-depressive SIBLING are themselves manic-depressive. If this is true, then assuming that identical twins have identical heredity and that most siblings do not, heredity must be an IMPORTANT factor in the cause of manic-depression. While most siblings do not have identical heredity, identical twins do. Hence, hereditary factors are important in the causation of manic-depression.[37]

(A = Identical twins have identical heredity, B = Most siblings do not have identical heredity)

---

[36] Winter 1976, p. 1.
[37] See Franz J. Kallmann, *Heredity in Health and Mental Disorder* (New York: W. W. Norton & Company, Inc., 1953), p. 124.

219 There are arguments against the claim that cigarette smoking causes cancer. Consider this one:

> *If cigarettes do cause cancer, then the earlier a person starts to smoke and the more he smokes, the sooner he would be expected to get lung cancer. Yet while people are smoking earlier and more heavily with each generation, the peak age for lung cancer remains about the same.*[38]

Set out formally, the argument goes as follows:

> If CIGARETTES cause cancer, then if people smoke MORE today than in the past, the average age of persons who contract lung cancer today will be LOWER than in the past. Thus, cigarettes do not cause cancer, because although people do smoke more today than in the past, the average age of those contracting lung cancer is not any lower than it used to be.

220 If there is JUSTICE in this life, then there is no NEED for a future life. If, on the other hand, there is no justice in our earthly existence, then we have no reason to think that God is just. But if we do not have reason to believe God to be just, then there is no reason to think that he will provide a future life for us. Therefore, either there is no need for a future life or there is no reason to believe that God will provide such a life.[39]

(A = We have reason to think that God is just, P = There is reason to believe that God will provide us with a future life)

221 A *Newsweek* column by Pete Axthelm begins:

> *The strapping rodeo bull rider grabbed Jerry Jeff Walker's arm in a vicelike grip and stared angrily at the singer, who bore a beatific, faraway expression on his face. "Didn't you hear me, boy?" he*

---

[38] From *The Tobacco Controversy*, a pamphlet published by the Tobacco Institute, 1971, p. 8.

[39] This reasoning is advanced by David Hume in *An Inquiry Concerning Human Understanding* (Indianapolis, Ind.: The Bobbs-Merrill Co., Inc., 1955), pp. 150–51.

growled. "I told you to play that song about red-necks. Now play it. Fast."

Stoned and drunk and uncertain if he was in a honky-tonk in Austin or in Oklahoma City, Walker struggled to concentrate on his dilemma. If he played the song, which he knew the cowboy hated, he would probably be beaten up. If he refused the request, he would also be beaten up. Finally, he began to play. The cowboy hit him three times, smashed his guitar and left him bloody.[40]

Jerry Jeff's dilemma:

> If I PLAY the song, I will be BEATEN. And if I do not play it, I will be beaten. So, I will be beaten up.

222   Argument 222 indicates how Boyle's Law may be derived from the kinetic theory of gases.[41]

> The pressure exerted by a gas in a container RESULTS from the impacts of the molecules upon the containing walls and is quantitatively EQUAL to the average value of the total momentum that the molecules deliver per second to a unit square of the wall area. If this is so, then the pressure of a gas is INVERSELY proportional to its volume and is DIRECTLY proportional to the mean kinetic energy of its molecules. The mean kinetic energy of the molecules of a fixed mass of gas remains CONSTANT as long as the temperature remains constant. If the pressure of a gas is inversely proportional to its volume and directly proportional to the mean kinetic energy of its molecules, and if the mean kinetic energy of the molecules of a fixed mass of gas remains constant as long as the temperature is held constant, then the PRESSURE of a fixed mass of gas at a constant temperature will be inversely proportional to its volume. It follows from the above that the pressure of a fixed mass of gas at constant temperature is inversely proportional to the volume of the gas.

223   The verifiability criterion of meaning may be stated 'A sentence is meaningful if and only if it is either analytic or verifiable'. An advocate

---

[40] "Songs of Outlaw Country," *Newsweek,* April 12, 1976, p. 79.
[41] See Carl G. Hempel, *Philosophy of Natural Science* (Englewood Cliffs, N.J.: Prentice-Hall, Inc., 1966), p. 73.

of this criterion has difficulty explaining the status of the criterion itself. This problem is pointed out succinctly by 223 and in more detail by 224.

If the criterion is TRUE, it is MEANINGFUL. But if it is true, then it is not meaningful. Hence, it is not true.

224 EVERY true statement is meaningful. If this is so, then the verifiability criterion is MEANINGFUL if it is TRUE. If the criterion is true, then it is meaningful if and only if it is either ANALYTIC or VERIFIABLE. But it is neither analytic nor verifiable. This proves that it is not true.

225 Candy's father's dilemma:

CANDY will not go to the party unless we take TOMAS. But Mrs. Viking will be RESENTFUL if we bring Tomas or if Candy does not attend. Hence [whether Tomas attends or not], Mrs. Viking will be resentful.

MARY WORTH by Allen Saunders and Ken Ernst. © Field Enterprises, Inc., 1972.

226 The following argument expresses the main theme of a CBS television special on the plight of private higher education in America:

Unless government heavily SUBSIDIZES private colleges, private higher education will CEASE to exist. But if government does subsidize private schools heavily, these schools will come under GOVERNMENTAL control. If the government controls the private schools, private higher education will no longer exist. Therefore, private higher education will cease to exist.

227 From Plato's *Meno:* [42]

Socrates: . . . *Then came the question whether virtue is acquired by teaching?*

Meno: *Yes.*

S: *If virtue was knowledge, then, as we thought, it was taught?*

M: *Yes.*

S: *And if it was taught it was knowledge?*

M: *Certainly.*

S: *And if there were teachers, it might be taught; and if there were no teachers, not?*

M: *True.*

S: *But surely we acknowledged that there were no teachers of virtue?*

M: *Yes.*

S: *Then we acknowledged that it was not taught, and was not knowledge?*

M: *Certainly.*

The argument formalized:

If virtue is KNOWLEDGE, then it is TEACHABLE. If it is teachable it is knowledge. If there are INSTRUCTORS of virtue it is teachable, and if there are no such instructors it is not teachable. But there are no instructors of virtue. It follows that virtue is not teachable and is not knowledge.

[42] 98d-e, Jowett translation.

228 The King reasons that Sir Rodney's making the bet is sufficient proof that Rodney loses.

> Rodney's WINNING the bet would show that gambling has not been completely ELIMINATED. Ergo Rodney loses. For he wins if and only if it has been eliminated.

THE WIZARD OF ID by permission of Johnny Hart and Field Enterprises, Inc. (October 24, 1973).

229 An engineer on a supertanker explains the need for a constant supply of distilled water on his ship.

> *If you haven't got the water, you can't flash the boiler. If you can't flash the boiler, you haven't got the steam for the engines, or for the alternators, which make the electricity. This is the chain reaction that leads to complete disaster. If there's not enough water on this ship, the ship stops.*[43]

The engineer's explanation formalized:

> If you haven't got the distilled WATER, you can't FLASH the boiler. If you can't flash the boiler, you haven't got the steam for the ENGINES or for the ALTERNATORS. No steam for the engines means that the ship STOPS. No steam for the alternators means no electrical POWER. Accordingly, if there is no distilled water, the ship will stop and will have no electricity.

230 A stanza from *The Recovery of Jerusalem* by the sixteenth-century Italian poet Tasso:

---

[43] Noël Mostert, "Supertankers—I," *The New Yorker*, May 13, 1974, p. 83. Reprinted by permission.

My lord, a double conquest must you make,
  If you achieve renown by this emprise:
For if our fleet your navy chase or take,
  For want of victuals all your camp then dies;
Or if by land the field you once forsake,
  Then vain by sea were hope of victories:
Nor could your ships restore your lost estate;
For steed once stolen, we shut the door too late.[44]

The stanza advances an argument.

You will be VICTORIOUS only if both your ARMY and your NAVY conquer, for these reasons. If your navy does not conquer, your army will STARVE. If your army starves, it will not conquer. And, finally, unless your army conquers, you will not be victorious.

231 The *sense-datum theory* maintains that what a person perceives directly are mental entities (sense data) rather than physical objects. One of the main arguments for the existence of sense data may be set out in the following way:

I see a rose that APPEARS pink to me. The rose is RED. If I see a rose that appears pink to me, then there is SOMETHING pink that I am seeing.[45] Now the rose cannot be both red and PINK. If there is something pink that I am seeing but the rose is not pink, then the rose is not the pink thing that I am seeing. If the rose is not the pink thing that I am seeing, then there exists a pink sense DATUM that I am seeing. It follows that there is a pink sense datum that I am now seeing.

(X = The rose is the pink thing that I am seeing)

232 In an episode of NBC television's *Sanford and Son*, Fred thinks he has accidentally shot his neighbor Goldstein. He and his son Lamont argue about who will go across the street to see. Fred says:

If I go and find him dead, I'll have a heart attack. If I go and find him alive, I'll jump around for joy and have a heart attack. So either way, if I go, I go.

[44] Book II, stanza lxxii, Fairfax translation. Note the inverted grammar of the third line.

[45] This is a highly doubtful premise. See Winston H. F. Barnes, "The Myth of Sense-Data," *Proceedings of the Aristotelian Society*, XLV (1944–45), 89–117.

The conclusion of this argument is 'If I GO to Goldstein's house, I will have a HEART attack'. (A = Goldstein is alive, J = I will jump around for joy)

233 One way to prove that someone is advancing an invalid argument is to produce a second argument that has exactly the same logical form as the first and that, in addition, has obviously true premises and an obviously false conclusion. The rationale of this procedure (which may be called "refutation by logical analogy") is set out by 233.

> Validity is wholly a matter of FORM. Our two arguments have the SAME form. If all of this is so, then YOUR argument is valid if and only if MINE is valid. My argument has true PREMISES and a false CONCLUSION. It cannot have both true premises and a false conclusion and be valid. Thus, your argument is invalid.

(C = My argument has a false conclusion)

234 A community newspaper story:

> *The question, "What's bugging you?" is not taken lightly at Naranja Lakes Elementary School. They've been going a little buggy—in the true sense of the word.*
>
> *The school . . . has neither air conditioning nor window screens and is surrounded by an illegal dumping area and a stagnant canal 20 feet from the school building.*
>
> *Where there is no air conditioning in Florida, there is heat.*
>
> *Where there is heat, there are open windows.*
>
> *Where there are open windows and no screens, there is easy access for all manner of flying and crawling life.*
>
> *And where there are dumping grounds and stagnant canals, there is an overabundance of mosquitoes, gnats, rats and many other undesirables.*[46]

This explanation of the prevalence of insects can be recast as an argument.

[46] Catherine Grim, "Kids Are 'Bugged' at Naranja Lakes," *The Guide* (Coral Gables, Florida), August 15, 1974, p. 1.

Naranja Lakes Elementary School has neither AIR conditioning nor window SCREENS and is surrounded by a DUMP and a stagnant CANAL. If the school lacks air conditioning, the school rooms will be HOT. Classroom windows will be OPEN if the rooms are hot. If the windows are open and screenless, insects will have access to the classroom. The dump and stagnant canal surrounding the school are a sufficient condition for the existence of MANY insects in the vicinity. Provided that there are many insects in the area and that they have access to the classrooms, there are INSECTS in the classrooms. Therefore, there are insects in the classrooms.

(B = insects have access to the classrooms)

235 The *ontological argument* for the existence of God was advanced by St. Anselm in the eleventh century. Anselm presented two versions of this argument, one of which may be formalized:

God is a being a greater than which cannot be conceived. It is possible to conceive of a being that cannot be conceived not to exist. If this is possible and if God can be conceived not to exist, then we can conceive of a being that is greater than God. But if we can conceive of a being greater than God, God is not a being a greater than which cannot be conceived. If God cannot be conceived not to exist, then he must exist. Thus, God exists.

Use these symbols:

G = God is a being a greater than which cannot be conceived
P = It is possible to conceive of a being that cannot be conceived not to exist
C = God can be conceived not to exist
W = We can conceive of a being greater than God
E = God exists

236 From Boswell's *The Life of Samuel Johnson:*

I described to him an impudent fellow from Scotland, who . . . maintained that there was no distinction between virtue and vice. JOHNSON. "Why, Sir, if the fellow does not think as he speaks, he is lying; and I see not what honor he can propose to himself from

*having the character of a lyar. But if he does really think that
there is no distinction between virtue and vice, why, Sir, when he
leaves our houses let us count our spoons."* [47]

Johnson's argument:

The Scot MAINTAINS that there is no distinction between virtue
and vice. If he maintains this but does not BELIEVE it, then
he is a LIAR. And if he is a liar he is not an HONORABLE
person. But if he does believe that there is no distinction
between virtue and vice, in that case also he is not an
honorable individual. Thus, Sir, he is not an honorable person.

237   Philosopher Edward Erwin writes:

In The Logic of Modern Physics, *Bridgman provided at most only a
few operational definitions; most of the concepts he employed in
that work were not defined at all. Thus, if it were true that we do
not know the meaning of a concept until it has been operationally
defined, we and Bridgman would fail to understand most, if
not all, of what was said in* The Logic of Modern Physics. *But
Bridgman's work was understood, as is shown by the great influence
it enjoyed; therefore, it is not true that to be intelligible, every
concept must be operationally defined.* [48]

Erwin's argument formalized:

Only a few of the concepts in Bridgman's book are DEFINED.
If this is so, then at most a few of them are OPERATIONALLY
defined. If it were true that every INTELLIGIBLE concept is
operationally defined, then if no more than a few of the
concepts in Bridgman's book are operationally defined, it
would follow that (at best) only a FEW of the concepts in the
book are intelligible. But the book has had GREAT influence.
If only a few of the concepts in the book were intelligible, then
the book could not have had great influence. Therefore, it is
not true that every intelligible concept is operationally defined.

[47] July 6, 1763.
[48] *The Concept of Meaninglessness* (Baltimore, Md.: Johns Hopkins University
Press, 1970), p. 12.

238   There are two numbers whose sum is 75 such that the first is larger than the second by 15. What are they? Read no further if you want to solve this simple puzzle on your own. The Russian mathematician Boris Kordemsky gives a solution and a proof in this passage:

> *Suppose that the second number is not 30. Then it is either greater than 30 or less than 30. If it is greater than 30, the first number is greater than 45 and their sum is greater than 75, which is impossible. If it is less than 30, the first number is less than 45, and their sum is less than 75, which is also impossible.*
>
> *Therefore, the second number is 30.*[49]

Kordemsky's proof is so nearly a fully explicit deductive argument that you should have little trouble symbolizing it. Treat the first two sentences as one conditional premise. Use these symbols:

A = The second number is 30
B = The second number is greater than 30
C = The second number is less than 30
D = The first number is greater than 45
E = The sum of the two numbers is greater than 75
F = The first number is less than 45
G = The sum of the two numbers is less than 75

239   Many passages in Plato's dialogues are devoted to showing defects in definitions of general terms. In the dialogue *Euthyphro*, for example, Plato (in the person of Socrates) attacks this definition of 'piety': *piety means what is pleasing to the gods.*[50] His criticism is paraphrased by 239. (Some of the premises in this argument seem absurd to us, but they would not have appeared so to Plato's contemporaries.)

The gods QUARREL. If they quarrel at all, then they quarrel over what is JUST and good. Anyone is PLEASED by what he thinks just and good, and DISPLEASED by what he thinks unjust and bad. If one is pleased by what he thinks just and good and displeased by what he thinks unjust and bad, and if the gods quarrel over what is just and good, then ONE thing

[49] *The Moscow Puzzles* (New York: Charles Scribner's Sons, 1972), puzzle 276.
[50] 6e–8a.

can please one god while displeasing another. If one thing can please one god and displease another, and if *piety* MEANS what is pleasing to the gods, then one thing can be BOTH pious and impious. Thus, *piety* does not mean what is pleasing to the gods, because one thing cannot be both pious and impious.

240   Boswell once wrote to Dr. Johnson as follows:

> *I earnestly desire tranquility . . . but fear I shall never attain it; for, when unoccupied I grow gloomy, and occupation agitates me to feverishness.*[51]

The conclusion is stated first. Supply this unstated premise: 'If I am GLOOMY or FEVERISH, I am not TRANQUIL'. (O = I am occupied)

241   In a television mystery movie, the detective cites three propositions to the murder suspect:

> If the cleaning lady CLEANED the room, then there would be no SCRAPS and no NEWSPAPER.
>
> If she did not clean, then there would be both scraps and a newspaper.
>
> There was a newspaper, but no scraps.

The detective then says to the suspect, "You see the contradiction, don't you, sir?" Demonstrate that the three propositions are contradictory by showing that they entail 'The cleaning lady cleaned the room but she did not clean it'.

242   Philosopher David E. Cooper writes:

> *The general point is this: If predicates are names of entities, then subject/predicate sentences are pairs of names, since subjects are names (or referring expressions). But a pair of names is not a sentence at all; it is a mere list. Hence one of the expressions in a subject/predicate sentence cannot be a name. Since subjects certainly do name, then predicates cannot.*[52]

[51] January 8, 1778.
[52] *Philosophy and the Nature of Language* (London: Longman Group Ltd., 1973), p. 93.

One plausible formalization of Cooper's argument:

> If both SUBJECTS and PREDICATES are names, then a subject/predicate sentence is a pair of NAMES. A pair of names is not a sentence. If a subject/predicate sentence is a pair of names and if a pair of names is not a sentence, then a subject/predicate sentence would not be a sentence. But, of course, a subject/predicate sentence IS a sentence. Subjects are names. It follows that predicates are not names.

($A =$ A pair of names is a sentence)

243 "The Sale of Philosophers" by the second-century author Lucian includes the following exchange between Stoic (a philosopher for sale) and Buyer:

> Stoic: *If your child wanders near a river, and a crocodile sees him and catches him, and then promises to give him back to you if you can tell him correctly what he has decided to do, give the child back or not—what would you say he'd decided to do?*
>
> Buyer: *That's a tricky question. I don't know what I'd say to get the child back. For heavens sake, you answer and save my child— quick, before the crocodile swallows him!* [53]

Stoic does not answer, but, as the following argument proves, Buyer ought to guess that the crocodile has decided to eat the child:

> Either the crocodile has decided to EAT the child or he has decided to RETURN it. If the latter, the child is SAVED. If the crocodile has decided to eat the child and Buyer GUESSES so, then in this case also the child is saved. Therefore, provided that Buyer guesses that the crocodile has decided to devour the child, the child is saved.

244 Either evolutionary theory is mistaken or I will not survive my death, in light of the following reasons. If EVOLUTIONARY theory is correct, then there exists an ancestral CHAIN that leads from me back to some very primitive organism [call it

[53] Lucian, *Selected Works* (Indianapolis, Ind.: The Bobbs-Merrill Co., Inc., 1965), p. 105.

"a"]. This "a" did not survive its death. If there is an ancestral chain linking me to "a," then if "a" did not survive its death but I shall survive mine, SOMEWHERE in the chain there was an animal that survived death even though neither of its parents did. And, finally, it cannot be true that there was an animal in the chain that survived death while its parents did not.

(A = "a" survived death, I = I shall survive death, S = Somewhere in the chain was an animal that survived death while its parents did not)

245 As her trial for speeding neared, a University of Miami coed began to worry that the outcome might interfere with her plans. Argument 245 defines her problem. (An unusual feature of this argument is its use of all five of the standard statement connectives.)

I will either PAY a fine or ATTEND traffic school. I will attend traffic school if and only if it is not on the WEEKEND. If I pay a fine and it is a HEAVY one, I cannot GO to Walt Disney World. So, if the fine is a heavy one and if traffic school is on the weekend, I will not be going to Walt Disney World.

246 (CHALLENGE) While a graduate student at M.I.T. in the late thirties, Claude Shannon discovered a remarkable parallel between electric switching circuits and propositional logic.[54] He found that a circuit can be represented by a logical formula in which (1) statement letters and their negations stand for switch positions, (2) the series connection of components is represented by conjunction, and (3) the parallel connection of components is represented by disjunction. On the basis of this correspondence one can simplify a switching circuit by means of the following steps:

(1) Represent the circuit by a logical formula.
(2) By logical techniques replace this formula by a second one that is simpler, yet logically equivalent to it.
(3) Translate the second formula into circuitry.

---

[54] See Shannon, "A Symbolic Analysis of Relay and Switching Circuits," *Transactions of the American Institute of Electrical Engineers*, LVII (1938), 713–23.

Consider an example:

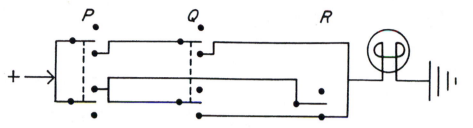

This circuit (C1) can be represented by formula F1:

(F1) Either both not *P* and not *Q*, or both *P* and either not *Q* or not *R*.

F1 is logically equivalent to the simpler formula F2:

(F2) Either not *Q* or both *P* and not *R*.

F2 translates into circuitry as C2:

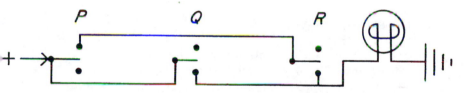

These two electric circuits are functionally equivalent (that is, they do the same job), yet C2 has only three switch components while C1 has five.

One claim in this account needs support—the claim that F1 and F2 are logically equivalent. They are equivalent if and only if F1 entails F2 (argument 246) and F2 entails F1 (247). Check the validity of these arguments.

F1. So, F2.

Use these symbols: *P, Q, R.*

247 (CHALLENGE)

F2. So, F1.

248 (CHALLENGE) In "The Dilemma of Determinism," William James draws out some unfortunate consequences of determinism.[55] Argument 248 paraphrases his reasoning.

> Murders are COMMITTED and REGRETTED. If murder is not BAD, then JUDGMENTS of regret are not correct. If DETERMINISM is true, then if murders occur and are bad, SIN is a necessary part of the world. If determinism is correct, then if murders are regretted and judgments of regret are mistaken, ERROR is a necessary feature of the world. Hence, if determinism is correct, then either sin or error is a necessary part of the world.

249 (CHALLENGE) Some universities have the following policy concerning the travel expenses of persons interviewed for faculty vacancies:

> The school pays if and only if it is not the case that both the school makes an offer and the applicant refuses the job.

Argument 249 reveals the rationale for such a policy.

> The school PAYS if and only if it is not the case that both the school makes an OFFER and the applicant REFUSES the job. If not offering the job is a sufficient condition for the school to pay, then the policy discourages the school from interviewing persons the school is not genuinely interested in hiring. If the job's being offered and turned down is a sufficient condition for the school not to pay, then the policy discourages applicants who are not genuinely interested in the job from interviewing. Therefore, the policy discourages the school from interviewing a person in whom it is not genuinely interested, and it also discourages applicants not really interested in the school from interviewing.

(A = The policy discourages the school from interviewing persons it is not genuinely interested in, B = The policy discourages applicants not genuinely interested in the job from interviewing)

250 (CHALLENGE) During a drive to unionize teachers at Kent State University, antiunion forces circulated a flyer containing these warnings:

[55] In *Essays in Pragmatism*, ed. Alburey Castell (New York: Hafner Publishing Co., Inc., 1948), p. 50.

If the union WINS the election and enforces an AGENCY shop, then you will have to PAY a fee of $135 per year or you will LOSE your job.

If the union wins the election and does not establish an agency shop but REQUIRES membership in order to vote, then you must pay a membership fee of $135 per year or you will be DISEN-FRANCHISED.

If the union wins the election and neither establishes an agency shop nor requires the payment of an annual membership fee in order to vote, then its power base will be UNDERCUT, and the union will be ineffective.

Show that the three warnings entail this statement:

If the union wins the election and is EFFECTIVE, then you will lose your job or be disenfranchised unless you pay a fee of $135 per year.

As the scale of the balance must give way to the weight that presses it down, so the mind must of necessity yield to demonstration.

Cicero

2·4 Natural Arguments

Each passage contains a propositional argument. In some cases a premise or conclusion is unstated and must be supplied. Extraneous material should be ignored.

251 "Your honor says, I am either a knave or a madman; now, as I'll assure your honor I am no knave, it follows that I must be mad."

> Tobias Smollett, *Humphrey Clinker* (New York: The New American Library, Inc., 1960), p. 144.

252 "STATE COLLEGE, Pa.—The wife of Penn State coach Joe Paterno denied published reports last night that her husband had signed to coach the New England Patriots of the National Football League.

" 'If Joe had signed a contract, I think he'd tell me first,' Mrs. Sue Paterno said. 'He hasn't told me. He hasn't signed any contract.' "

> "Paterno's Wife Denies Signing" (Associated Press), *Miami News*, January 6, 1972, p. 1-B.

253

> October 8, 1968, King Features Syndicate, Inc.

254   "If there be righteousness in the heart,
       there will be beauty in the character.
If there be beauty in the character,
       there will be harmony in the home.
If there be harmony in the home,
       there will be order in the nation.
If there be order in the nation,
       there will be peace in the world."

> Confucius, *The Great Learning*, quoted in Houston Smith, *The Religions of Man* (New York: Harper & Row, Publishers, 1958), p. 160.

255   "And if, for example, antiabortionism required the perverting of natural reason and normal sensibilities by a system of superstitions, then the liberal could discredit it—but it doesn't, so he can't."

> Roger Wertheimer, "Understanding the Abortion Argument," *Philosophy and Public Affairs*, I (Fall 1971), 87.

256   "Naive realism, if true, is false; therefore it is false."

> Bertrand Russell, *An Inquiry into Meaning and Truth* (Harmondsworth, Middlesex: Penguin Books, Ltd., 1965), p. 13.

257 "Either nature is uniform or it is not. If nature is uniform, scientific induction will be successful. If nature is not uniform, then no method will be successful. [It follows that] if any method of induction will be successful, then scientific induction will be successful."

> Brian Skyrms, *Choice and Chance* (Belmont, Calif.: Dickenson Publishing Company, Inc., 1966), p. 39.

258 "Jews should *not* believe in Jesus unless He is the Messiah. . . . Jesus is the Messiah."

> Pamphlet published by "Jews for Jesus."

259

December 31, 1968, Washington Star Syndicate, Inc.

260 "We seem confronted, then, with a dilemma: either our choices have sufficient causal conditions or they do not; if they do have sufficient causal conditions they are not avoidable; if they do not, they are fortuitous . . . and therefore, since our choices are either unavoidable or fortuitous, we are not morally responsible for them."

> Roderick Chisholm, "Responsibility and Avoidability," in *Determinism and Freedom in the Age of Modern Science*, ed. Sidney Hook (New York: Collier Books, 1961), p. 158. (Chisholm discusses, but does not advance, this argument.)

261 In a segment of NBC's "Little House on the Prairie," Pa Ingalls is about to lose his brace of oxen to a greedy merchant. He says,

"If we lose the oxen, I can't make a crop. I can't make a crop and we lose everything." [56]

[56] The second sentence is a conditional.

262

© King Features Syndicate, Inc., 1972.

263 "At this point an annoying, though obvious, question intrudes. If Skinner's thesis is false, then there is no point in his having written the book or our reading it. But if his thesis is true, then there is also no point in his having written the book or our reading it."

Noam Chomsky, "The Case Against B. F. Skinner," *The New York Review of Books* (December 30, 1971), p. 20 Reprinted with permission from *The New York Review of Books.* Copyright © 1971 Nyrev, Inc.

264

THE WIZARD OF ID by permission of Johnny Hart and Field Enterprises, Inc. (March 23, 1977).

265

'OK, Mr. Press Secretary, give me some answers!'

'If I knew about the Watergate Caper, what am I doing in the White House?'

'. . And if I <u>didn't</u> know anything about the affair. . .'

'. . What am I doing in the White House?'

266 "Without the yak they [the Tibetans] could have no milk; without the milk they could have no butter; without the butter they could have no tea; without the tea they could have no existence. Selah. Without the yak they could have no plough; without the plough they could have no crop; without the crop they could have no food; without the food they could have no existence. Selah. Without the yak, they could have no loads; without the loads they could have no goods; without the goods they could have no barter; without the barter they could have no existence. Selah. Without the yak they could have no wool; without the wool they could have no money; without the money they could have no goods; without the goods they could have no existence. Selah."

George N. Patterson, *Tibetan Journey* (London: Faber & Faber, Ltd., 1954). Reprinted by permission of Faber & Faber Ltd. and W. W. Norton & Company, Inc. (American edition entitled *Journey with Loshay.*)

267

"I, for one, am glad the dollar's out of trouble, because if the dollar's in trouble, then the dime is certainly in trouble."

Drawing by Dana Fradon; © 1971 The New Yorker Magazine, Inc.

268   "The most familiar paradox is the following:

(S) This sentence is false.

It is reasonable to assume that (S) is either true or false. But if it is true, then, as it says, it is false. On the other hand, if the sentence is false, then, since it says it is false, it is true. Therefore, if the sentence is either true or false, then it is both true and false."

Keith Lehrer, *Knowledge* (Oxford: Clarendon Press, 1974), p. 25.

269

APARTMENT 3-G by Alex Kotzky. © Field
Enterprises, Inc., 1972. Courtesy of Field
Newspaper Syndicate.

270   "$A \supset B$ is false just in case A is true and B is false. . . . Therefore,
if A is true and if $A \supset B$ is true, B has to be true."

Karel Lambert and Bas C. van Fraassen,
Derivation and Counterexample (Encino
and Belmont, Calif.: Dickenson Publishing Company, Inc., 1972), p. 31.

CHAPTER THREE

Property Logic

It was a saying of the ancients, "Truth lies in a well"; and to carry on this metaphor, we may justly say that logic does supply us with steps, whereby we may go down to reach the water.

Isaac Watts

3·1 Symbolization Sentences

Letters for abbreviating predicates are usually indicated by printing certain words entirely in capitals. The first letter of such a word abbreviates the predicate that contains the word. For example, the predicate letters for exercise 271 are *G* and *H*. Letters for abbreviating singular terms are generally indicated by underscoring words. The first letter of such a word represents the singular term. For instance, in exercise 272, *s* symbolizes 'Sammy Davis, Jr.'

In some exercises it is convenient to employ a restricted *universe of discourse* (the class of objects dealt with in the exercise). These restricted universes are indicated in dictionaries.

271 "Some GERMS are HELPFUL."

Children's science book

272 "Sammy Davis, Jr. is JEWISH."

Newspaper

(s = Sammy Davis, Jr.)

273 "All SPORE-forming bacteria are GRAM-positive."

Biology text

(Sx = x is a spore-forming bacterium)

274 "Everybody is GUILTY."

Camus

(Universe: people)

275 "DEAD people don't LEAVE fingerprints."

Television detective

(Universe: people)

276 "CRUSTACEA possess a well-developed ENDOCRINE system."

Biology text

277 "There are no such things as WITCHES!"

Sitcom dialogue

278 "Many snake BITES are not FATAL."

First-aid pamphlet

279 "There are TRUTHS, at least one."

Philosopher Bernard Bolzano

280 "There has never been a person killed in Dade County wearing a shoulder harness and seat belt."

Newspaper

(Universe: people; Dx = x was killed in Dade County, Hx = x was killed while wearing a shoulder harness and a seat belt)

281 "Neither <u>Christ</u> nor <u>Buddha</u> had a LAWYER."

Novel

282 "Not all PROSTITUTES are JUNKIES."

Newspaper

283 "If it doesn't say AMANA it's not a RADAR range."

Advertisement

($Ax = x$ is labeled "Amana")

284 "There is a CARDINAL Tetra or a NEON Tetra in the tank."

Conversation

(Universe: fish in the tank)

285 "Only MEN go BALD."

J. R. Lucas

(Universe: people)

286 "A member of PARLIAMENT who behaves as a strictly HONEST man is REGARDED as a fool."

James Boswell

287 "There's no team in COLLEGE football that can't be BEATEN."

Coach Barry Switzer

(Universe: football teams; $Cx = x$ is collegiate, $Bx = x$ can be beaten)

288 "Everything GOOD in Christianity comes from either PLATO or the STOICS."

Bertrand Russell

($Gx = x$ is a good feature of Christianity)

289 "<u>Abdul</u>-Jabbar is BLACK and a MUSLIM, but not a Black Muslim."

Newspaper

($Cx = x$ is a Black Muslim)

290 "And in the south, only the states along the COAST will not have RAIN today."

Television weatherman

(Universe: southern states)

291 "MOORS are all of them CHEATS, FORGERS, and SCHEMERS."

Don Quixote

292 "EDUCABLE mentally RETARDED children lack a high level of generalization."

Special education text

(Universe: children; $Hx = x$ has a high level of generalization)

293 "Some of the motor NEURONS go to GLANDS rather than to MUSCLES."

Psychology text

($Nx = x$ is a motor neuron)

294 "Brockway Lecture Hall is open at all times that the library itself is not open."

Campus announcement

(Universe: moments; $Bx =$ Brockway is open at x, $Lx =$ the library is open at x)

295 "Some SLEEPWALKERS are carrying out suppressed or REPRESSED desires."

Psychology text

($Ax = x$ carries out a suppressed desire)

296 "Some HUSBANDS are IMPERIOUS and some WIVES PERVERSE."

Samuel Johnson

297 "The people who sin the sins of KALAMAZOO are neither SCARLET nor CRIMSON."

Carl Sandberg

(Universe: people; Kx = x sins the sins of Kalamazoo)

298 "All RESPIRING cells have MITOCHONDRIA but strictly FERMENTING cells do not."

Biology text

(Universe: cells)

299 "He whose TESTICLES are crushed or whose male MEMBER is cut off shall not ENTER the assembly of the Lord."

Deuteronomy 23:1

(Universe: people)

300 "There will be ENOUGH heating oil for everybody if everybody TURNS down the heat."

Advertisement

(Universe: people; Ex = there is enough heating oil for x)

301 "Every man I meet is either MARRIED, too YOUNG, or he WANTS to do my hair."

Doris Day

(Fx = x is a man, Gx = Doris Day meets x)

302 "A CATHOLIC who joins the MASONS FORFEITS his right to receive the sacraments, and he will be canonically EXCOMMUNICATED from the Catholic church."

"Dear Abby"

303 "If one manufacturer can MEET the pollution standards, none will be given an EXTENSION."

EPA spokesperson

(Universe: auto manufacturers)

304 "A child falls VICTIM to Tay-Sachs disease only if he inherits a Tay-Sachs gene from both his FATHER and MOTHER."

News magazine

(Universe: children)

305 "No COMMUNICABLE disease has ever been ERADICATED unless there was a preventive VACCINE to do so."

Health official

(Universe: diseases)

306 "There are OLD pilots and there are BOLD pilots—but there are no old bold pilots."

Sign in an Air Force ready room

(Universe: pilots)

307 "All FELONS in Minnesota except first-degree MURDERERS RECEIVE indeterminate sentences."

Newspaper

($Fx = x$ is a Minnesota felon)

308 (CHALLENGE) "My wife and I do not fly together unless our two children, Patricia and Ronald, accompany us."

Ronald Reagan

(Universe: airplane flights; Wx = Reagan's wife is on x, Rx = Reagan is on x, Sx = Reagan's son is on x, Dx = Reagan's daughter is on x)

309 (CHALLENGE) "LADIES and GENTLEMEN of the court CAUGHT sleeping with their boots on will be instantly DECAPITATED."

Peter the Great

310 (CHALLENGE) "Defining obscenity, [the bill states:] 'Material is OBSCENE if its predominant appeal is to PRURIENT interest and it is utterly without REDEEMING social value, and

if, in addition, it goes substantially BEYOND accepted limits
of candor.' "

Newspaper

What is gained by argument, is gained forever.
Wendell Phillips

3·2 Valid Arguments

311   Anyone who DELIBERATES about alternative courses of action
BELIEVES he is free. Everybody deliberates about alternative
courses of action. This shows that we all believe ourselves to
be free.[1]

(Universe: people)

312   When guru Baba Hari Dass visited Miami, someone asked him,
"Everybody's saying Miami is the spiritual capital of the world. Is that
true?" Dass, who has not spoken for 23 years, wrote: "If everybody says
it, then I say it." His reply expresses the following argument:

Everybody SAYS that Miami is the spiritual capital of the world.
So, <u>Dass</u> says it.

(Universe: people; $Sx = x$ says that Miami is the spiritual capital of the
world)

313   Newspaper item:

*WATERLOO, Iowa—Marva Drew, a 51-year-old Waterloo
housewife, has just finished typing every number from one to
one million.*

*It took five years and 2,473 pieces of typing paper to accept the
challenge of her son, Daryl, now 23, who came home from school*

---

[1] See James W. Cornman and Keith Lehrer, *Philosophical Problems and Arguments: An Introduction* (New York: The Macmillan Company, 1968), pp. 131–41.

one day and said a teacher had told the class no one could count up to one million.[2]

Thanks to Marva's efforts we can advance this argument:

<u>Marva</u> has COUNTED to one million. So, the claim that no one counts up to one million is false.

(Universe: people)

314 During a recent wave of gangland murders in New York City (applauded by some residents), the police commissioner assigned hundreds of policemen to the task of preventing further violence. He justified the action with the following argument: [3]

All human life is SACRED. Ergo, MOBSTERS' lives are sacred.

(Universe: human lives; $Mx = x$ is a mobster's life)

315 The detective's argument:

Since the horse who <u>kicked</u> the deceased wore CORKS, he could not have belonged to the JUDGE, because the judge's horses never wore corks.

($k =$ the horse who kicked the deceased)

April 8, 1977. Courtesy of Chicago Tribune–New York News Syndicate.

316 Some prison officials who take the view that the purpose of imprisonment is rehabilitation are troubled by the fact that people are im-

[2] "Proved a Point—by the Numbers," *Miami News*, December 9, 1974, p. 1-A.
[3] See "Gang War in New York May Be Bloodiest Yet," *Miami News*, April 17, 1972, p. 4-A.

prisoned for smoking marijuana. The following argument expresses their concern:

> A person can BE rehabilitated in prison only if he or she WANTS rehabilitation. MARIJUANA users do not want rehabilitation. So, they cannot be rehabilitated in prison.

(Universe: people)

317 When the California Supreme Court ruled that the state's system of financing education was illegal, it based its decision on the following argument: [4]

> California's system depends on LOCAL property taxes, and a system that depends on local property taxes DISCRIMINATES against the poor. Hence, California's system VIOLATES the Fourteenth Amendment, because any system that discriminates against the poor violates that amendment.

(Universe: systems of financing education; c = California's system)

318 MENTAL events are not BRAIN events. The proof: Mental events are private. Brain events are physical. Physical events are public. Public events are not private.

(Universe: events; Ax = x is private, Cx = x is a physical event, Dx = x is public)

319 Until recently, the state of Florida had a law that banned freak shows. When Stanley Berent, known as "Sealo the Seal Boy," appealed it, the State Supreme Court upheld his appeal, reasoning as follows: [5]

> The law banning freak shows DEPRIVES some people of the right to earn a living. There cannot be a CONSTITUTIONAL law that does that. Consequently, the law banning freak shows is unconstitutional.

(Universe: laws; l = the law banning freak shows)

320 Newspaper filler:

> *Not all of today's women devote all their waking thoughts to pleasing men. Some are married.*[6]

[4] "Exit the Property Tax?" *Newsweek*, September 13, 1971, p. 61.
[5] "Freak Show Ban Voided by Court," *Miami News*, October 12, 1972, p. 2-A.
[6] *Washington Star-News*, December 26, 1972, p. 11-C.

This quip involves an argument:

> MARRIED WOMEN do not DEVOTE all their waking thoughts to pleasing men. Some women are married. Thus, not all women devote all their waking thoughts to pleasing men.

($Dx = x$ devotes all her waking thoughts to pleasing men)

321   This World War II cartoon by Bill Mauldin suggests an argument.

> When we haven't caught them we MOVE. And when we do CATCH them we still move. So, we're always moving.

(Universe: moments; $Cx = x$ is a moment when we have caught the enemy, $Mx = x$ is a moment when we are moving)

"Hell. When they run we try to ketch 'em. When we ketch 'em we try to make 'em run."

Drawing copyrighted 1944, renewed 1972, Bill Mauldin; reproduced by courtesy of Bill Mauldin.

322 Members of the electoral college are either USELESS or DANGEROUS. The reason: they are useless if they do their JOB and dangerous if they do not.

(Universe: members of the electoral college)

323 The verifiability criterion of meaning was criticized in exercises 223 and 224. Another attack on the criterion: [7]

Some MEANINGFUL sentences lack truth values. Yet every VERIFIABLE sentence has a TRUTH value. Thus, the thesis that a sentence is meaningful if and only if it is verifiable is false.

(Universe: sentences)

324 Kant advances the following argument in *Foundations of the Metaphysics of Morals*: [8]

Every duty is either RIGOROUS or MERITORIOUS. All rigorous duties follow from the CATEGORICAL imperative, and so do all meritorious duties. Thus, all duties follow from the categorical imperative.

(Universe: duties; $Cx = x$ follows from the categorical imperative)

325 The philosopher J. L. Mackie employs this argument: [9]

TEMPORAL beings are not OMNIPOTENT. Neither are nontemporal beings. Consequently, <u>God</u> is not omnipotent.

326 Columnist James J. Kilpatrick, describing the report of the President's Commission on Obscenity and Pornography:

The commission's conclusion is based entirely upon this line of reasoning: In a free society, all conduct should be lawful which causes no demonstrable narm to others; empirical proof cannot be

[7] See G. J. Warnock, "Verification and the Use of Language," in Paul Edwards and Arthur Pap, *A Modern Introduction to Philosophy*, 3rd ed. (New York: The Free Press, 1973), p. 782.

[8] (Indianapolis, Ind.: The Bobbs-Merrill Co., Inc., 1959), p. 42.

[9] See "Evil and Omnipotence," *Mind*, LXIV (1955), 212.

adduced that pornography causes such harm; therefore the traffic in pornography should be lawful.[10]

(Universe: types of conduct; $Lx = x$ should be lawful, $Hx = x$ is known to be harmful, $Px = x$ is an instance of traffic in pornography)

327 An extract from an article on acne in a religious newspaper:

In fact, if you are a boy, your having acne might even be said to be something for which to be thankful. How so? you ask. In that, for one thing, it is evidence that you are not a eunuch. Eunuchs are not plagued with acne, for acne is triggered by the male or androgenic hormones.[11]

Bad-complexioned teenagers who wonder whether they are eunuchs can take heart! Their cloud is lined with silver, as the following argument demonstrates:

EUNUCHS do not have ACNE. It follows that no BOYS who have acne are eunuchs.

328 As an Israeli fighter pilot watched a man bail out of a crippled plane he reasoned:

The parachutist is the PILOT of an Egyptian fighter, and he has BLOND hair. EGYPTIANS are never blond. Any non-Egyptian pilot of an Egyptian fighter must be a RUSSIAN. Hence, some pilots of Egyptian fighters are Russians.

($p =$ the parachutist, $Px = x$ pilots an Egyptian fighter)

329 Percy and Flo reason:

Any moment is either BEFORE or AFTER the pub opens. Before opening time Andy is GROUCHY, and after opening time he has a HANGOVER. So, whatever the time, Andy is either grouchy or hungover.

---

[10] James J. Kilpatrick, "Danish Solution to Pornography" (Washington Star Syndicate, Inc.), *Miami Herald*, September 29, 1970, p. 7-A. Reproduced by permission.

[11] "Acne—the Teen-Ager's Woe," *Awake*, January 8, 1971, p. 17.

(Universe: moments; Gx = Andy is grouchy at time x, Hx = Andy has a hangover at time x)

Daily Mirror Newspapers Ltd. ANDY CAPP by Reggie Smythe ® Dist. Field News-paper Syndicate (January 8, 1974).

330   Abby scores again:

> *DEAR ABBY:*
>
> *Between you and me, the people who write to you are either morons, or they're just plain stupid.*
>
> *—HARRY IN ST. LOUIS*
>
> *Which are YOU?* [12]

Her inference:

> <u>Harry</u> WROTE to "Dear Abby." Consequently, if the people who write to "Dear Abby" are either MORONIC or STUPID, Harry is one or the other.

(Universe: people)

331   In *The Principles of Human Knowledge,* Berkeley advances many arguments against the belief that there are material objects. In one he maintains that everything can be explained without assuming the exist-ence of material bodies. He concludes as follows:

> *If therefore it were possible for bodies to exist without [that is, outside of] the mind, yet to hold that they do so must needs be a*

---

[12] Abigail Van Buren, "Dear Abby" (Chicago Tribune—New York News Syn-dicate, Inc.), *Miami News,* March 28, 1973, p. 8-B. Reproduced by permission.

very precarious opinion, since it is to suppose, without any reason at all, that God has created innumerable beings that are entirely useless and serve to no manner of purpose.[13]

This argument can easily be formalized.

If MATERIAL objects exist, they have no use. GOD would not create anything that is entirely USELESS. Thus, there are no material objects, since any material object would be God's creation.

($Ux = x$ is useless, $Gx = x$ is created by God)

332 No PERFECT being is immoral. Any individual who fails to value intellectual honesty is imperfect. No MORAL individual who VALUES intellectual honesty would punish AGNOSTICISM. It follows that if <u>God</u> is perfect he will not punish agnosticism.

333 A zero-sum game is one in which a gain for one side entails a corresponding loss for the other; poker is such a game. Obviously, not everyone can win in a zero-sum game. Argument 333 makes this point.

Someone WINS only if someone does not. Therefore, it is false that everyone wins.

(Universe: people)

334 Philosopher Carl Hempel writes:

If the terms and principles of a theory serve their purpose they are unnecessary, as just pointed out; and if they do not serve their purpose they are surely unnecessary. But given any theory, its terms and principles either serve their purpose or they do not. Hence, the terms and principles of any theory are unnecessary.[14]

(Universe: theories; $Sx =$ the terms and principles of x serve their purpose, $Ux =$ the terms and principles of x are unnecessary)

---

[13] (Indianapolis, Ind.: The Bobbs-Merrill Co., Inc., 1957), p. 32.
[14] "The Theoretician's Dilemma," in *Aspects of Scientific Explanation* (New York: The Free Press, 1965), p. 186. Hempel rejects the first premise of this, the "theoretician's dilemma."

335 Logic texts commonly say that *any* argument having the form 'If *p* then *q; q;* therefore *p'* (affirming the consequent) is invalid. This is a mistake; some arguments that have this form are valid. Argument 335 is an example.[15]

> If something is RED, everything is red. Everything is red. Therefore, something is red.

336 Argument 335 affirms the CONSEQUENT; nevertheless it is VALID. So, it is false that all arguments that affirm the consequent are invalid.

(Universe: arguments; a = argument 335)

337 From a collegiate newspaper:

> *For the first time ever, UM students will elect a woman Student Body President in runoff elections today in the Student Union Breezeway. . . .*
>
> *The candidates for president are Susan Havey and Kathy McPhee.*[16]

The reporter reasoned deductively,

> A WOMAN will be elected PRESIDENT, because either Havey or McPhee will be elected and both are women.

338 The most famous argument *against* the existence of God is the argument from evil, which can be formulated:

> If there is a PERFECT being, he is omniscient, omnipotent, and ALL good. If there is an omniscient, omnipotent, and all good being, then there will be no natural catastrophes. Since NATURAL catastrophes do occur, there must not be a perfect being.

($Yx = x$ is omniscient, $Zx = x$ is omnipotent)

---

[15] For a discussion of this mistake and similar ones see James Willard Oliver, "Formal Fallacies and Other Invalid Arguments," *Mind*, LXXVI (1967), 463–78. Argument 335 is Oliver's example.

[16] Alan Marcus, "Students to Vote in USBG Runoff for Top Offices," *Miami Hurricane*, April 6, 1976, p. 1.

339 An aloof professor at the University of Richmond has office hours from seven to eight in the morning. His reason:

> Students who NEED to confer with me will COME to my office [even at that hour], but those who do not need to confer will not come. Thus, a student will come to my office if and only if he needs to confer with me.

(Universe: students)

340 If the following syllogism is tested with one of the standard techniques of syllogistic logic (the Venn diagram test, for example), it will be judged invalid.[17] It commits the "fallacy" of drawing an affirmative conclusion from a negative premise. Quantificational logic permits a deeper analysis of the argument; such analysis shows the argument to be valid. Can you spot the peculiar characteristic of the argument that guarantees its validity? (Hint: See 95.)

> Some TALL men are not MORTAL. All men are mortal. Therefore, all men are tall men.

(Universe: men)

341 A second example of a valid argument that will test out "invalid" under the techniques of syllogistic logic:

> No MEN are IMMORTAL. No TALL men are immortal. So, all tall men are men.

Exercise 478 may help you see why this unpersuasive argument is formally valid.

342 From a newspaper story:

> "A rape, under Florida law, is characterized by force and penetration. . . . If [either of] those two elements [is] not present, the rape did not occur," said Lt. Norris.[18]

---

[17] This exercise is based on an example given by James Willard Oliver in "Formal Fallacies and Other Invalid Arguments," *Mind*, LXXVI (1967), 472.

[18] Lynn Feigenbaum, "Half of Rape Cases Labeled Unfounded," *Miami News*, February 1, 1975, p. 4-A.

The first statement (the premise) may be viewed as definitional and so may be symbolized as a (universally quantified) biconditional. ($Rx = x$ is a rape, $Fx = x$ involves force, $Px = x$ involves penetration)

343 I Kings, chapter 18 (verses 20 to 40) describes a contest on Mt. Carmel between Elijah and 450 prophets of Baal. Elijah regards the result of the contest as a demonstration of the divinity of Jehovah. His reasoning:

> A god is GOD if and only if he answers his prophets by FIRE. This proves that <u>Jehovah</u> is God and <u>Baal</u> is not, for Jehovah but not Baal answers by fire.

(Universe: gods; $Gx = x$ is God)

344 In the *Leviathan*, Thomas Hobbes reasons: [19]

> UNDERSTANDING involves LANGUAGE. Accordingly, if only MEN use language, then only men understand.

($Ux = x$ understands, $Lx = x$ uses language)

345 Philosopher David Hume writes:

> *Whatever is distinct, is distinguishable; and whatever is distinguishable, is separable by the thought or imagination. All perceptions are distinct. They are, therefore, distinguishable, and separable.*[20]

($Ax = x$ is distinct, $Bx = x$ is distinguishable, $Sx = x$ is separable, $Px = x$ is a perception)

346 A writer for *The New York Review of Books* relates a conversation with Tim Galloway, author of *Inner Tennis*:

> *I ask Galloway how he had come to believe Maharaj Ji was God.*
>
> *"When I first heard him my only approach was to say to myself, 'He's either the real thing or a con artist.' Well the first times I saw him he just did too bad a job as a con artist. A good con artist*

[19] (Chicago, Ill.: Henry Regnery Co., 1956), p. 38.
[20] *A Treatise of Human Nature* (Oxford: The Clarendon Press, 1888), p. 634.

wouldn't wear a gold wrist watch or give such stupid answers. When I was staying with him in India I once asked him how much time I should spend on work and how much on meditation and he just said get up an hour earlier and go to bed an hour later, hardly a profound answer. I decided that if he was doing such a bad job of being a holy man he simply had to be genuine."

"Did it ever occur to you that he might be a bad *con man?"*

"Then how could he have six million followers?" the tennis pro replied.[21]

Galloway's argument:

<u>Maharaj</u> Ji is either GOD or a good or BAD con artist. A good con artist would not WEAR a gold wrist watch or give STUPID answers, both of which Maharaj Ji does. And a bad con artist would not have six million FOLLOWERS, like Maharaj Ji. Thus, Maharaj Ji is God.

($Gx = x$ is God, $Ax = x$ is a good con artist, $Bx = x$ is a bad con artist)

347   Winston Churchill offers the following explanation of why Japanese cabinets in the decade prior to World War II were heavily influenced by the military:

The Army and Navy Ministers of the Cabinet had to be respectively a general and an admiral on the active list. If a Prime Minister could not find a general or an admiral to hold these offices he could not form or maintain a Cabinet, and professional spirit was so strong that no general or admiral would serve as Army or Navy Minister in a Cabinet whose policy was strongly disapproved of by his Service. Thus the Army and Navy Staffs were able to exert a continual, and at times decisive, influence on policy by withdrawing, or threatening to withdraw, the Service Ministers from a Cabinet.[22]

Churchill's explanation reformulated as a deductive argument:

All cabinets have an ARMY and a NAVY minister. But a cabinet

---

[21] Francine du Plessix Gray, "Blissing Out in Houston" (December 13, 1973), p. 37. Reprinted with permission from *The New York Review of Books.* Copyright © 1973 Nyrev, Inc.

[22] *The Second World War,* Vol. III: *The Grand Alliance* (New York: Bantam Books, Inc., 1962), p. 491.

whose policy is disapproved by the Army does not have an Army minister. And a cabinet whose policy is disapproved by the Navy does not have a Navy minister. Hence, no cabinet has a policy that is disapproved by either the Army or the Navy.

(Universe: pre-World War II Japanese cabinets; Bx = the Army disapproves of the policy of x, Cx = the Navy disapproves of the policy of x)

348 The philosopher Antony Flew has argued that religious utterances (for example, 'God is love') are, strictly speaking, meaningless.[23] The bones of his reasoning are represented by 348.

All MEANINGFUL nonanalytic statements are (in principle) FALSIFIABLE. Hence, RELIGIOUS statements are not meaningful, since they are neither ANALYTIC nor (in principle) falsifiable.

(Universe: statements)

349 The philosopher of religion John Hick disagrees with the first premise of the preceding argument.[24] His criticism runs on the order of 349.

Any statement that is (in principle) VERIFIABLE is MEANINGFUL. The <u>sentence</u> 'Somewhere there is a stone that weighs more than five pounds' is (a) nonanalytic, (b) (in principle) verifiable, and (c) not (even in principle) FALSIFIABLE. So, it is false that all meaningful nonanalytic statements are (in principle) falsifiable.

(Universe: statements; s = the sentence 'Somewhere there is a stone that weighs more than five pounds', Ax = x is analytic)

350 Logic students sometimes doubt the claim that all conditional sentences (sentences of the form "if p then q") with false antecedents (the "p" part) are true. Argument 350 shows that this claim is a logical consequence of the standard ascription of truth conditions to the conditional, taken together with an obvious logical truth.

---

[23] See Flew's "Theology and Falsification," in *New Essays in Philosophical Theology*, ed. Antony Flew and Alasdair MacIntyre (London: Student Christian Movement Press, 1955).
[24] See Hick, "Theology and Verification," *Theology Today*, XVII (1960), 12–31.

A conditional is true if and only if it does not have a true
antecedent and a false consequent. No conditionals with false
antecedents have true antecedents. Therefore, all conditionals
with false antecedents are true.

(Universe: conditionals; $Jx = x$ is true, $Kx = x$ has a true antecedent, $Lx = x$ has a false consequent, $Mx = x$ has a false antecedent)

351 The nature of mathematics has been a matter for philosophical dispute for centuries. Arguments 351 through 353 give the briefest of outlines for three views advanced on this subject by (among others) John Stuart Mill, A. J. Ayer, and Immanuel Kant. Argument 351 reflects Mill's position.[25]

MATHEMATICAL propositions have CONTENT. Only
SYNTHETIC propositions have content. There are no synthetic
a priori propositions.[26] Every proposition is either a priori or
a posteriori. It follows that mathematical propositions are
synthetic a posteriori.

(Universe: propositions; $Bx = x$ is a priori, $Dx = x$ is a posteriori)

352 MATHEMATICAL propositions are NECESSARY. A posteriori
propositions are not necessary. There are no SYNTHETIC
a priori propositions. Every proposition is either synthetic or
ANALYTIC, and either a priori or a posteriori. So, mathematical
propositions are analytic a priori.[27]

(Universe: propositions; $Dx = x$ is a posteriori, $Bx = x$ is a priori)

[25] See Mill's *A System of Logic, Rationative and Inductive* (New York: Harper & Brothers, Publishers, 1859), Bk. II, Chs. 5–7.

[26] This premise is a cardinal principle of empiricism. It is accepted by Ayer, also, but is rejected by Kant. Rough definitions for the four technical terms employed in 351 through 353:

analytic means true (or false) by virtue of the meanings of terms;
synthetic means not analytic;
a priori means independent of experience;
a posteriori means dependent on experience.

For more adequate definitions of these four terms and a discussion of the nature of mathematics, see Stephen F. Barker, *Philosophy of Mathematics* (Englewood Cliffs, N.J.: Prentice-Hall, Inc., 1964).

[27] See A. J. Ayer, *Language, Truth and Logic* (Harmondsworth, Middlesex: Penguin Books Ltd., 1971), ch. 4.

353   MATHEMATICAL propositions are NECESSARY. Only a priori
propositions are necessary. Mathematical propositions have
CONTENT. Only SYNTHETIC propositions have content.
Therefore, mathematical propositions are synthetic a priori.[28]

(Universe: propositions; $Bx = x$ is a priori)

354   This argument establishes a logical principle that is employed in
exercise 489.

If the PREMISE set of an argument is not contradictory but its
CONCLUSION *is* contradictory, then it is LOGICALLY possible
that all of its premises are true and its conclusion false. No
argument for which this is a logical possibility is VALID. Hence,
any valid argument that has a contradictory conclusion also
has a contradictory premise set.

(Universe: arguments; $Px = x$ has a contradictory premise set, $Cx = x$
has a contradictory conclusion, $Lx =$ it is logically possible that the
premises of x are true and the conclusion of x false)

355   Logician Geoffrey Hunter writes:

*A tautology is a formula that can be checked to be true for all
interpretations by the usual (finite) truth-table method. Some
logically valid formulas of the predicate language Q cannot be so
checked.*[29]

The conclusion of this argument is unstated but can be readily supplied.
The first premise is a definition; as such it should be symbolized as a
(universally quantified) biconditional. (Universe: formulas; $Tx = x$ is a
tautology, $Cx = x$ can be checked to be true for all interpretations by the
usual truth-table method, $Vx = x$ is logically valid, $Qx = x$ belongs to the
predicate language Q)

---

[28] See Immanuel Kant, *Critique of Pure Reason* (New York: St. Martin's Press,
Inc., 1961), pp. 52–53.
       [29] *Metalogic* (Berkeley and Los Angeles, Calif.: University of California Press,
1971), p. 60.

356 Morris Kline on the Greeks' discovery of irrationals:

> *The fact which must be faced squarely is that an irrational is a new kind of number. It is a number because it expresses quantity, for example, the length of the hypotenuse of a right triangle. It is a new kind of number because the Pythagorean proof shows that an irrational number cannot equal a whole number or a fraction.*[30]

Kline's argument formalized:

> Proof that IRRATIONALS are NUMBERS that were new to the GREEKS: (1) An irrational expresses QUANTITY, (2) only numbers express quantity, (3) an irrational is neither WHOLE nor a FRACTION, (4) any number that is neither whole nor a fraction was new to the Greeks.

357 If no one CONTRIBUTES to Care, then someone PERISHES from hunger. Therefore, there is a person who perishes from hunger if *he* does not contribute to Care.

It seems obvious that this argument is invalid. Nevertheless, when it is symbolized in the standard fashion, the symbolization is found valid. Prove that the symbolized version of 357 is valid. (Universe: people)

358 The Salem authorities SPARED a person accused of witchcraft if and only if he or she "CONFESSED" to being a witch. All the accused who "confessed" to being witches when they were not actually WITCHES PERJURED themselves. Only those accused who "confessed" to being witches perjured themselves. Of course, none of the accused actually was a witch. This means that the authorities spared all the accused who perjured themselves and only those accused who perjured themselves.

(Universe: Salemites accused of witchcraft; $Wx = x$ was a witch)

359 When Dade County, Florida, enacted a clear meat-packaging ordinance, the County Attorney, after researching the matter in *Web-*

---

[30] *Mathematics and the Physical World* (New York: Thomas Y. Crowell Company, 1959), p. 45.

ster's Dictionary, ruled that the ordinance did not apply to chicken.[31] Don't cluck until you consider his argument.

> The ORDINANCE applies to all MEAT but only to meat. Meat [by definition] is ANIMAL flesh used as FOOD, excluding fish flesh and fowl flesh. But CHICKEN flesh is fowl flesh. So, the ordinance does not apply to chicken.

($Bx = x$ is fish flesh, $Dx = x$ is fowl flesh)

360   (CHALLENGE) Roderick Chisholm offers this formalization of a major deterministic argument.

> *1. If a choice is one we could not have avoided making, then it is one for which we are not morally responsible.*
>
> *2. If we make a choice under conditions such that, given those conditions, it is causally . . . impossible for the choice not to be made, then the choice is one we could not have avoided making.*
>
> *3. Every event occurs under conditions such that, given those conditions, it is causally . . . impossible for that event not to occur.*
>
> *4. The making of a choice is the occurrence of an event.*
>
> *5. [Therefore] we are not morally responsible for any of our choices.*[32]

Use these symbols:

$Cx = x$ is a choice
$Ax = x$ is avoidable
$Rx = x$ involves moral responsibility
$Nx = x$ is causally necessary
$Ex = x$ is an event

[31] "Metro Finds Package Law Fowl-safe," *Miami News,* June 28, 1973, p. 8-A.
[32] "Responsibility and Avoidability," in *Determinism and Freedom in the Age of Modern Science,* ed. Sidney Hook (New York: Collier Books, 1961), p. 157.

Note that "x's occurrence is causally necessary" is equivalent to "it is causally impossible for x not to occur."

People generally quarrel because they cannot argue.

G. K. Chesterton

3·3 Valid and Invalid Arguments

This exercise set may be supplemented by exercises 41 through 100. Note that the method of treating singular terms in syllogistic logic differs from the one used in predicate logic. For example, in symbolizing exercise 46, abbreviate 'the earth' with e.

361   Andy's date reasons:

Andy has a neatly DARNED scarf. Any man with a neat darn in his scarf is MARRIED. It follows that Andy is married.

(Universe: men; $Dx = x$ has a neatly darned scarf)

© Daily Mirror Newspapers Ltd. ANDY CAPP by Reggie Smythe ® Dist. Field Newspaper Syndicate (April 13, 1973).

362   A television detective discovers an earring in a trunk from which an antique dagger has been taken. Presumably the earring was dropped by

the thief. When the trunk's owner claims that the thief is the ghost of her dead sister, the detective replies, "In my limited experience with ghosts, they don't wear earrings." The detective's argument:

> The <u>thief</u> wore EARRINGS. Thus, the thief is not a GHOST, since ghosts don't wear earrings.

363 When insurance comes to you with imagination it comes to you from INA. So, all INA insurance comes to you with imagination.

($Ax = x$ is insurance that comes to you with imagination, $Ix = x$ is INA insurance)

364 The prehistoric mouse reasons from the facts:

> This <u>cavewoman</u> went UP, but she did not come DOWN. This disproves the theory that what goes up must come down.

(c = this cavewoman)

B.C. by permission of Johnny Hart and Field Enterprises, Inc. (December 19, 1973).

365 Nick Thimmesch writes in a *Newsweek* column on abortion:

> *To those considering the fetus as an organ, like, say a kidney, Dr. Andre Hellegers of Georgetown University pointed out that fetuses have their own organs and cannot be organs themselves.*[33]

[33] "The Abortion Culture," July 9, 1973, p. 7.

Dr. Hellegers' argument:

> The FETUS is not an ORGAN, because organs do not HAVE
> organs, and fetuses do.

($Hx = x$ has an organ)

366 The philosophers S. I. Benn and R. S. Peters maintain that causal
explanations are inadequate for much human behavior.[34] This argument
paraphrases one of their reasons.

> Some human behavior is RULE following. Rule-following
> behavior cannot be explained adequately in terms of CAUSES.
> Consequently, some human behavior cannot be adequately
> explained causally.

(Universe: human behavior; $Cx = x$ can be adequately explained
causally)

367 Roy Hayes's novel, *The Hungarian Game*, includes this telephone
conversation:

> *"Harry's used magazines. If we ain't got it, it ain't worth readin'."*
>
> *"I'm looking for an issue of* Forbes. *The July . . . ."*
>
> *"It ain't worth readin'."* [35]

As an argument, this can be read two ways. Maybe the clerk at Harry's
has drawn the following inference:

> A magazine that Harry's does not HAVE is not WORTH reading.
> Thus, JULY issues of *Forbes* are not worth reading, since
> Harry's does not have any of them.

(Universe: magazines)

---

[34] See chapter nine of *Social Principles and the Democratic State* (London:
George Allen & Unwin, Ltd., 1959).

[35] (New York: Simon & Schuster, Inc., 1973).

368 Perhaps the clerk has drawn this inference:

A magazine that Harry's does not HAVE is not WORTH reading.
No JULY issues of *Forbes* are worth reading. Consequently,
Harry's does not have any of them.

(Universe: magazines)

369 Many people (especially authors of high-school English texts)
maintain that a valid deductive argument is one that proceeds from the
general to the specific and that a correct inductive argument proceeds
from the specific to the general.[36] We will concentrate on the first half of
this claim (the part dealing with deduction). Arguments 369 through
371 do not proceed from the general to the specific. So, if any one of
them is deductively valid, the abovementioned claim is mistaken. Argument 369 is an example of passing from general to general.

All CATS are MAMMALS. Hence, all cats are either mammals
or REPTILES.

370 This argument is an example of passing from specific to specific.

Jones is a TALL ALCOHOLIC. So, Jones is tall.

371 This argument passes from specific to general.

Brown is a REPUBLICAN LABOR leader. It follows that some
labor leaders are Republicans.

372 In *The Praise of Folly*, Erasmus says:

*Christ himself in the Gospel denies, that anyone is to be called good
but one, and that is God. And then if he is a fool that is not wise,
and every good man according to the Stoics is a wise man, it is no
wonder if all mankind be concluded under folly.*[37]

---

[36] For a refutation of both parts of this claim see Brian Skyrms, *Choice and
Chance* (Belmont, Calif.: Dickenson Publishing Co., Inc., 1966), pp. 13–15.
[37] *The Praise of Folly*, trans. John Wilson (Ann Arbor, Mich.: The University
of Michigan Press, 1958), p. 129.

The following seems to be Erasmus's argument:

> No men are GOOD. He is a FOOL that is not WISE. Every good man is a wise man. Hence, all men are fools.

(Universe: men)

373   Dialogue in Plato's *Phaedo*:

> Socrates: . . . *Tell me, what must be present in a body to make it alive?*
>
> Cebes: *Soul.*
>
> Socrates: *Is this always so?*
>
> Cebes: *Of course.*
>
> Socrates: *So whenever soul takes possession of a body, it always brings life with it?*
>
> Cebes: *Yes, it does.*[38]

Socrates advances (and Cebes accepts) this argument:

> Every live BODY has a SOUL. So, every body that has a soul is ALIVE.

374   In 1954 in the case of "Brown versus the Board of Education of Topeka," the Supreme Court ruled unanimously that school segregation was unconstitutional. The heart of the reasoning contained in their opinion is represented by the following inference:

> Any instance of school segregation VIOLATES the Fourteenth Amendment for these reasons: All school segregation GENERATES feelings of inferiority among members of the minority group. Any school segregation that does this treats students UNEQUALLY. Any school segregation that treats students unequally is a violation of the Fourteenth Amendment.

(Universe: instances of school segregation)

[38] 105c–105d, Hugh Tredennick translation.

375 All LUTHERANS are PROTESTANTS. Therefore, some Lutherans are Protestants.

376 Analyze 375 using "Lutherans" as the universe of discourse. If you get discrepant results, can you account for them? ($Px = x$ is a Protestant)

377 Charlie reasons:

> This <u>letter</u> is not a TRAFFIC citation, as it was sent to a DOG, and no letter sent to a dog is a traffic citation or a summons to JURY duty.

(Universe: letters)

© 1973 United Feature Syndicate, Inc.

378 An advertisement posted on collegiate bulletin boards reads "Jaguar by Yardley has insured you for $10,000 (in case you're maimed, mauled, trampled and dismembered by 50 or more frenzied females)." Sophomore Gerald Swindle conceived the idea of paying the girls of Pi Upsilon $2,000 to maul and trample him in a frenzied manner. However, he gave the idea up—partly as a result of his logical researches. Obviously he was toying with argument 378.

> Anyone maimed, mauled, TRAMPLED, and DISMEMBERED by 50 or more frenzied females is ELIGIBLE to collect $10,000 from Yardley. Gerald <u>Swindle</u> was mauled and trampled by 50 or more frenzied females. Therefore, he is eligible to collect $10,000 from Yardley.

(Universe: men; $Yx = x$ is maimed by 50 or more frenzied females, $Zx = x$ is mauled by . . . females, $Tx = x$ is trampled by . . . females, $Dx = x$ is dismembered by . . . females)

379 In the play, *The King and I*, the King of Siam sings the following lines:

Shall I join with other nations in alliance?
If allies are weak am I not best alone?
If allies are strong with power to protect me,
Might they not protect me out of all I own?

.   .   .

Is a puzzlement! [39]

The king has sung an argument.

> Every potential ally of Siam is either WEAK or STRONG. Weak allies are USELESS. But a strong ally would pose a THREAT. Thus, any potential ally is either useless or threatening.

(Universe: Siam's potential allies; $Ux = x$ is useless)

380   A famous passage from Joseph Heller's *Catch-22*:

> *Group Headquarters was alarmed, for there was no telling what people might find out once they felt free to ask whatever questions they wanted to. Colonel Cathcart sent Colonel Korn to stop it, and Colonel Korn succeeded with a rule governing the asking of questions. Colonel Korn's rule was a stroke of genius, Colonel Korn explained in his report to Colonel Cathcart. Under Colonel Korn's rule, the only people permitted to ask questions were those who never did. Soon the only people attending were those who never asked questions.*[40]

This argument explains why Colonel Korn's rule stopped the questions:

> The only people PERMITTED to ask questions are those who do not ASK questions. And clearly, those who are not permitted to ask questions do not ask any. Thus, no one asks questions.

(Universe: people attending the sessions)

381   Descartes thought the human soul was connected to the body at the pineal gland. One could argue for this thesis with 381. (The third premise was accepted by Descartes, although it is now known to be false.)

---

[39] "A Puzzlement." © 1951 by Richard Rogers and Oscar Hammerstein II.
[40] Copyright © 1955, 1961 by Joseph Heller. Reprinted by permission of Simon & Schuster, a Division of Gulf & Western Corporation.

There is an ORGAN in the human body where the soul joins the body. Any organ where the human body and the soul are joined must be one that animals lack. Consequently, the <u>pineal</u> gland is an organ in the human body where the soul and body intersect, since ANIMALS do not possess this gland.

($Ox = x$ is an organ in the human body where the soul joins the body, $Ax = x$ is an organ that animals possess)

382   G. E. Moore writes in his paper, "A Defence of Common Sense":

When I speak of "philosophers" I mean, of course (as we all do), exclusively philosophers who have been human beings. . . . If, therefore, there have been any philosophers, there have been human beings.[41]

($Px = x$ is a philosopher, $Hx = x$ is a human being)

383   In *Language, Truth and Logic*, A. J. Ayer reasons: [42]

No proposition that has FACTUAL content can be NECESSARY. Accordingly, either all MATHEMATICAL propositions lack necessity or they all lack factual content.

(Universe: propositions)

384   If <u>God</u> has FOREKNOWLEDGE of everything, then no person has free WILL. Consequently, God cannot have both foreknowledge of everything and free will.

(Universe: persons; $Fx = x$ has foreknowledge of everything)

385   The Mauldin cartoon suggests this argument.

Anybody who's not PARANOID in WASHINGTON is CRAZY. Since paranoid people are crazy, all Washingtonians are crazy.

(Universe: people)

[41] *Contemporary British Philosophy*, 2nd series, ed. J. H. Muirhead (London: George Allen and Unwin, 1924), p. 202.
[42] (Harmondsworth, Middlesex: Penguin Books Ltd., 1971), p. 97.

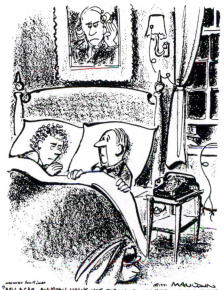

"MY DEAR, ANYBODY WHO'S NOT PARANOID IN WASHINGTON IS CRAZY."

March 3, 1971, Chicago Sun-Times Syndicate.

386   An editorial in *The Miami News* charged that only the children of influential people were enrolled in the University of Miami's laboratory school. A parent replied to this charge in a letter to the editor.[43] Argument 386 reproduces her reasoning.

> Certainly University President Stanford has INFLUENCE; yet he was unable to enroll his child in West Lab. Therefore, it is false that only persons with influence get their children ENROLLED.

(Universe: people; Ex = a child of x is enrolled in West Lab)

387   The philosopher and mathematician Frege believes that there exists, in addition to the physical and mental realms, a third realm that contains propositions.[44] One of his arguments for this view is paraphrased by 387.

[43] See "A Parent Defends West Lab School," *Miami News,* January 24, 1969, p. 12-A.

[44] See Gottlob Frege, "The Thought: A Logical Inquiry," trans. by A. M. and Marcelle Quinton, *Mind,* LXV (1956), 289–311.

There are propositions. They are SHARABLE but not perceivable by the senses. Nothing in the MENTAL realm is sharable. Everything in the PHYSICAL realm is perceivable by the senses. Therefore, there exist entities belonging neither to the physical realm nor to the mental realm.

($Ax = x$ is a proposition, $Bx = x$ is perceivable by the senses)

388 Legendary college football coach Jake Gaither (Florida A & M) gives this advice to coaches:

> *If you haven't got it, you should sing the blues. That way, if you lose, the fans will say "he told you that before the season." And if you win, they'll think you're a heckuva coach.*[45]

Jake's argument:

> The coach of a mediocre team who sings the BLUES is EXCUSED by the fans if he does not have a WINNING season. And he is PRAISED by the fans if he does have a winning season. It follows that the fans either praise or excuse the coach of a mediocre team who sings the blues.

(Universe: coaches of mediocre teams)

389 We were discussing the concept of "event" in an introductory philosophy class and considering the question whether *thinking about a girlfriend* should be counted as an event. A student who thought it should advanced the following argument (using some of my remarks for his first two premises):

> Every EVENT occurs in TIME. Nothing that has WEIGHT is an event. Thus, thinking about a GIRLFRIEND is an event, because it occurs in time but lacks weight.

($Gx = x$ is an instance of thinking about a girlfriend)

390 Logician Geoffrey Hunter writes:

> *By 28.3 every theorem of PS is a tautology of P, and by the semantic completeness theorem for PS every tautology of P is a*

[45] John Crittenden, "Gaither's Farewell: The Books Balance," *Miami News,* August 1, 1973, p. 1-E.

theorem of PS. So a formula of P is a theorem of PS iff [if and only if] it is a tautology of P.[46]

(*Ax* = *x* is a theorem of *PS*, *Bx* = *x* is a tautology of *P*, *Fx* = *x* is a formula of *P*)

391 Any integer LARGER than zero is POSITIVE. And any integer SMALLER than zero is NEGATIVE. But zero is neither larger nor smaller than itself. Consequently, zero is neither positive nor negative.

(Universe: integers; *Lx* = *x* is larger than zero, *Sx* = *x* is smaller than zero, *k* = zero)

392 When a ban was imposed in Dade County, Florida, on detergents containing phosphate, dishwasher detergents were exempted. The Pollution Control Board made this exception in light of the following argument:

> There are no nonphosphate DISHWASHER detergents.[47] Hence, if all PHOSPHATE detergents were BANNED, then all dishwasher detergents would be banned.

(Universe: detergents)

393 Mrs. Shick was not much good at kitten sexing, but she could reason:

> Either all of Smudgie's kittens are MALES or all are FEMALES [as they all look alike in the relevant respects]. Some of the kittens are CALICOES. All calicoes are females. Therefore, all of Smudgie's kittens are females.

(Universe: Smudgie's kittens)

394 The philosopher of science Ernest Nagel writing about scientific explanation:

> *Explanations are not invariably judged to be unsatisfactory unless*

---

[46] *Metalogic* (Berkeley and Los Angeles, Calif.: University of California Press, 1971), pp. 118–19.
[47] True at the time (1971).

*they effect a reduction of the unfamiliar to the familiar. When the
bleaching effect of sunlight on colored materials is explained in
terms of physical and chemical assumptions about the composition
of light and of colored substances, the explanation is not rejected
as unsatisfactory, even though it is the familiar which is being
accounted for in terms of what to most men is quite unfamiliar.*[48]

Nagel's reasoning formalized:

It is not true that explanations are invariably unsatisfactory
unless they REDUCE the unfamiliar to the familiar. This is
shown by the fact that the explanation of the bleaching effect
of sunlight is not unsatisfactory, even though it does not
reduce the unfamiliar to the familiar.

(Universe: explanations; b = the explanation of the bleaching effect of
sunlight, $Sx = x$ is satisfactory)

395 The logicians Terrell and Baker include a symbolized version of
395 in a set of (purportedly) valid arguments.[49] Does it belong there?

If either everything is C or everything is M, then nothing is D.
Some things are both D and E. Therefore, something is neither
C nor M.

396 Either all of the HOUSES being built across the street will be
sales MODELS or none will be models. Some of those houses
are being built under FHA. No models are built under FHA.
So, none of the houses going up across the street will be
models.

($Hx = x$ is a house being built across the street, $Fx = x$ is built under
FHA)

397 Some philosophers have maintained that all meaningful words are
names. Argument 397 criticizes this view.[50]

[48] *The Structure of Science* (New York: Harcourt, Brace & World, Inc., 1961),
p. 46.

[49] See D. B. Terrell and Robert Baker, *Exercises in Logic* (New York: Holt,
Rinehart & Winston, Inc., 1967), p. 177, problem 2. Also compare problems 3 and
4 on p. 175.

[50] This argument is based on a discussion by Gilbert Ryle in "The Theory of
Meaning," in *British Philosophy in the Mid-Century*, ed. C. A. Mace (London:
George Allen & Unwin, Ltd., 1957), p. 244.

If every WORD is a NAME, then every SENTENCE that CONTAINS more than one word is a LIST. Lists do not have TRUTH values. It follows that some words are not names, since some sentences do have truth values.

398   The medieval theologian and philosopher Odo Rigaud wrote:

Everything habitual which exists in the intellective part [of the soul] as a disposition is either a virtue or a science. Theology is such a habit. Since it is not a virtue, it is obvious it must be a science.[51]

($Hx = x$ is a habit, $Ix = x$ is in the intellective part of the soul, $Dx = x$ is a disposition, $Vx = x$ is a virtue, $Sx = x$ is a science, $t =$ theology)

399   (CHALLENGE)

Whatever exists is material. So, exactly one of the following two claims is true: (1) nothing is mental; (2) some material things are mental, and all mental things are material.

($Ax = x$ is material, $Bx = x$ is mental)

400   (CHALLENGE)

A syllogism that has a universal conclusion distributes the minor term in the conclusion. A valid syllogism that distributes the minor term in the conclusion distributes that term in its premise set. Every valid syllogism has at least one distributed middle term. If a syllogism distributes its middle term at least once and also distributes the minor term in its premise set, it will have more than one term distributed in its premise set. All valid syllogisms that have affirmative conclusions have two affirmative premises. No syllogism with two affirmative premises and a particular premise will have more than one term distributed in the premise set. Any syllogism with a universal negative conclusion distributes both the minor term and the major term in the conclusion. A syllogism that distributes both the minor and major terms in the conclusion is valid only if it distributes both those terms in the premise set. Any valid syllogism has at least one distributed middle

[51] "Theological Questions," in *Medieval Philosophy*, ed. John F. Wipple and O. F. M. Wolter (New York: The Free Press, 1969), p. 267.

term. Any syllogism that distributes both the major and minor terms in its premise set and in addition has at least one distributed middle term will distribute more than two terms in its premise set. Every valid syllogism has at least one affirmative premise. No syllogism that has a particular premise and at least one affirmative premise will have more than two terms distributed in its premise set. Any syllogism that has a universal conclusion will have either an affirmative or a negative conclusion. A syllogism has a particular conclusion if and only if it does not have a universal conclusion. Hence, any valid syllogism with a particular premise has a particular conclusion.

(Universe: syllogisms; $Ax = x$ has a universal conclusion, $Bx = x$ distributes the minor term in the conclusion, $Vx = x$ is valid, $Cx = x$ distributes the minor term in its premise set, $Dx = x$ has at least one distributed middle term, $Ex = x$ has more than one term distributed in its premise set, $Fx = x$ has an affirmative conclusion, $Gx = x$ has two affirmative premises, $Hx = x$ has a particular premise, $Ix = x$ has a negative conclusion, $Jx = x$ distributes both the minor and the major terms in the conclusion, $Kx = x$ distributes both the minor and the major terms in its premise set, $Lx = x$ has more than two terms distributed in its premise set, $Mx = x$ has at least one affirmative premise, $Nx = x$ has a particular conclusion)

Logic is the anatomy of thought.
John Locke

3·4 Natural Arguments

This exercise set may be supplemented by exercises 101 through 110.

401 "A really sensible person wouldn't have a jester. So anyone who has a jester is not sensible."

Diderot, *Rameau's Nephew* (Harmondsworth, Middlesex: Penguin Books, Ltd., 1971), p. 83.

402

THE WIZARD OF ID by permission of Johnny Hart and Field Enterprises, Inc. (May 19, 1975).

403 "For animal meat to be kosher the animal has to have split hooves and chew its cud. The pig does not chew its cud so it is not kosher, or 'terefah.'"

> Bob Wilcox, "Keeping Kosher: A Serious Matter," *Miami News*, January 15, 1970, p. 7-C.

404 "If an ampliative inference could be justified deductively it would not be ampliative. It follows that ampliative inference cannot be justified deductively."

> Wesley Salmon, *The Foundations of Scientific Inference* (Pittsburgh, Pa.: University of Pittsburgh Press, 1967), p. 11.

405 "Beautiful people see and enjoy things, and for that reason we know that Mr. and Mrs. Edward M. Miller of Hollywood are beautiful people."

> "Life With Larry Thompson," *Miami Herald*, January 11, 1973, p. 10-E.

406 "AS4.1, however, commits us to saying that some propositions *are* necessarily necessary; for it asserts that all necessary propositions are necessarily necessary, and in any system containing AS4.1 there must be some necessary propositions at least."

> G. E. Hughes and M. J. Cresswell, *An Introduction to Modal Logic* (London: Methuen and Co. Ltd., 1968), p. 269.

407 "Moreover, all things that exist, in so far as they exist, are true. . . . We have already shown that the soul seeks all true . . . things. Hence it seeks all things."

> Marsilio Ficino, "Platonic Theology," trans. J. L. Burroughs, in *The Portable Renaissance Reader*, ed. James Bruce Ross and Mary Martin McLaughlin (New York: The Viking Press, Inc., 1968), p. 390.

408 "If anything is supremely one it must be supremely being and supremely undivided. Now both of these belong to God. . . . Hence it is manifest that God is 'one' in the supreme degree."

> St. Thomas Aquinas, *Summa Theologica,* First Part, Question 11, Article 3.

409 "We may . . . define a metaphysical sentence as a sentence which purports to express a genuine proposition, but does, in fact, express neither a tautology nor an empirical hypothesis. And as tautologies and empirical hypotheses form the entire class of significant [meaningful] propositions, we are justified in concluding that all metaphysical assertions are nonsensical [meaningless]."

> A. J. Ayer, *Language, Truth and Logic* (Harmondsworth, Middlesex: Penguin Books Ltd., 1971), p. 56.

410 "Our judgements about our actual duty in concrete situations [lack] certainty. . . . A statement is certain . . . only in one or other of two cases: when it is either self-evident, or a valid conclusion from self-evident premises. And our judgements about our particular duties have neither of these characters."

> W. D. Ross, *The Right and the Good* (Oxford: The Clarendon Press, 1930), p. 30.

CHAPTER FOUR

Relational Logic

> *Nay, Sir, argument is argument. You cannot help paying regard to their arguments, if they are good.*
>
> Samuel Johnson

4·1 Symbolization
Sentences

As in chapter three, letters for abbreviating predicates are usually indicated by printing certain words in capitals. If the predicate is relational, a subscript R is appended to the capitalized word. For example, in exercise 411 Mxy symbolizes 'x is married to y'. Most of the relational predicates in the chapter are dyadic (two-place). When a predicate is triadic its abbreviation is specified in a dictionary.

411   "<u>Frank</u> and <u>Gloria</u> are MARRIED$_R$ but not LIVING$_R$ together."

"No, no, it's Frank and Gloria who are married but not living together. George and Judy are living together but not married."

Drawing by Chon Day; © 1972 The New Yorker Magazine, Inc.

412   "Some people FEAR$_R$ everyone."

Psychology text

(Universe: people)

413   "There's always somebody TOUGHER$_R$ than you."

College football player

(Universe: people)

414   "Nobody's LOWER$_R$ than <u>Carlton</u>."

Billboard

(Universe: cigarette brands; $Lxy = x$ has less tar than y)

415   "No one is LIKED$_R$ by everyone."

Newspaper

(Universe: people; $Lxy = x$ likes y)

416 "Each of us is lonely some of the time."

Philosopher Abraham Kaplan

($Px = x$ is a person, $Lxy = x$ is lonely at time y)

417 "The <u>Lord</u> ACCEPTS$_R$ all who accept Him."

Short story

(Universe: persons)

418 "All LIFE COMES$_R$ from something living."

The law of biogenesis

($Lx = x$ is living)

419 "No DETERGENT GETS$_R$ out everything."

Television advertisement

420 "There are more germs in the mouth of a human than in the mouth of any animal."

Letter to "Dear Abby"

($Gxy = x$ has more germs than y, $Hx = x$ is a human mouth, $Bx = x$ is a brute's mouth)

421 "Not all STUDENTS are APATHETIC$_R$ about everything."

College newspaper

422 "There's no chain LOCK that someone couldn't BREAK$_R$."

Newspaper

($Px = x$ is a person)

423 "Everything <u>God</u> CREATED$_R$ for man's good, <u>Satan</u> PERVERTS$_R$ for man's harm."

Billy Graham

($Cxy = x$ creates y for man's good, $Pxy = x$ perverts y for man's harm)

424 "The sun does not SHINE$_R$ all the time anywhere."

Newspaper

(Sxy = the sun shines at place x at time y)

425 "Any player with an AGENT$_R$ is a professional."

NCAA ruling

(Fx = x is a player, Axy = x is agent of y, Gx = x is a professional)

426 "Not all MODELS are AVAILABLE$_R$ at every STORE."

Radio advertisement

427 "Nobody but a FOOL is ever RUDE$_R$ to a good DOCTOR."

Doctor Dolittle

(Universe: people; Dx = x is a good doctor)

428 "The best MAN who ever breathed isn't GOOD$_R$ enough for the worst WOMAN in the world."

"My Little Chickadee"

(Mx = x is a man, Gxy = x is good enough for y, Wx = x is a woman)

429 "A SOLID body FLOATS$_R$ on a LIQUID if its specific GRAVITY$_R$ is less than that of the liquid."

College textbook

(Gxy = the specific gravity of x is less than that of y)

430 "Not every WOMAN has a CRUSH$_R$ on her DOCTOR$_R$."

"Dear Abby"

(Dxy = x is y's doctor)

431 "To some SURGEONS, any WOMAN OVER 35 is fair game for a hysterectomy."

Medical critic Dr. Sidney Wolfe

(Hxy = x regards y as fair game for a hysterectomy)

432   "The King of <u>Siam</u> SENT$_R$ AMBASSADORS to <u>Louis</u> XIV, but Louis XIV sent none to the King of Siam."

Samuel Johnson

($Sxyz = x$ sends y to z)

433   "A Manchu EMPEROR could COHABIT$_R$ only with a MANCHU."

Television documentary

($Ex = x$ was a Manchu emperor, $Cxy = x$ was permitted to cohabit with y)

434   "Not all WELFARE groups COOPERATE$_R$ all the time."

Newspaper

($Cxyz = x$ cooperates with y at time z)

435   "Somebody's lying about everything—or everybody's lying about something."

Magazine

($Lxy =$ person x is lying about y)

436   "An ENEMY$_R$ of an enemy is a FRIEND$_R$."

Arab proverb

(Universe: people; $Exy = x$ is an enemy of y)

437   "I OWE$_R$ nothing to anyone, nobody owes anything to <u>me</u>."

Thomas Mann's *The Wardrobe*

($Oxyz =$ person x owes y to person z)

438   "There's no STATE where a GAY can practice MEDICINE$_R$ or LAW$_R$."

Newspaper

($Mxy = x$ can practice medicine in y, $Lxy = x$ can practice law in y)

439   "Though there is never a day when everything is in bloom, there is never a day when something isn't in bloom."

Newspaper story about a tropical garden

(*Bxy* = flowering plant *x* is in bloom on day *y*)

440   "For every MUSCLE that BENDS$_R$ a JOINT there is one that STRAIGHTENS$_R$ it."

Children's book

441   "Seville—of all SPANISH towns is none more PRETTY$_R$."

Byron's *Don Juan*

(Universe: towns; *Pxy* = *x* is prettier than *y*)

442   "If an OBSERVATION report CONFIRMS$_R$ a certain sentence, then it also confirms every sentence which is logically EQUIVALENT$_R$ with the latter."

Philosopher Carl Hempel

(Universe: sentences)

443   "A CONJUNCTION is TRUE just when all of its conjuncts are true."

Logic text

(*Axy* = *x* is a conjunct of *y*)

444   (CHALLENGE) "No one UNDER junior high school age is ADMITTED, unless accompanied by a PARENT$_R$."

Newspaper

(Universe: people; *Bxy* = *x* accompanies *y*)

445   (CHALLENGE) "An EMPIRICAL finding is RELEVANT$_R$ for a HYPOTHESIS if and only if it constitutes FAVORABLE$_R$ or UNFAVORABLE$_R$ evidence for it."

Philosopher Carl Hempel

446 (CHALLENGE) "A PERSON BARRED$_R$ from one pari-mutuel ESTABLISHMENT in Florida is barred from all."

Newspaper

($Bxy = x$ bars y, $Ex = x$ is a Florida pari-mutuel establishment)

447 (CHALLENGE) "A BOY RESPECTS$_R$ a GIRL who doesn't SLEEP$_R$ with every fellow in town."

Letter to "Dear Abby"

(Universe: people in town)

448 (CHALLENGE) "If the NCAA is going to investigate every college BASKETBALL team that had at least one ineligible player, <u>Tufts</u> will wind up as the national CHAMPION."

Sports attorney

($Nx =$ the NCAA investigates x, $Ex = x$ is eligible, $Pxy = x$ plays on team y, $t =$ the Tufts basketball team)

449 (CHALLENGE) "No matter what an AMERICAN MOTHER COOKS$_R$, she's not HAPPY unless some American SON is forced to EAT$_R$ it."

MOMMA by Mell Lazarus. Courtesy of Mell Lazarus and Field Newspaper Syndicate.

450 (CHALLENGE) "[Technically,] a brother-in-law is either the BROTHER$_R$ of one's spouse or the HUSBAND$_R$ of one's sister."

Newspaper

($Lxy = x$ is brother-in-law of y, $Axy = x$ is spouse of y, $Cxy = x$ is sister of y)

*Testimony is like an arrow shot from a longbow;
the force of it depends on the strength of the
hand that draws it. But argument is like an arrow
from a cross-bow, which has equal force if
drawn by a child or a man.*

Robert Boyle

4·2 Valid Arguments

451 Maharaj Ji LOVES$_R$ everybody. So, he loves himself.

(Universe: people)

452 Mark Twain said, "There is somebody who is smarter than anybody —and that's everybody." The statement preceding the dash is false if construed literally (which is not the way Twain intended it), as argument 452 demonstrates.

> Nobody is SMARTER$_R$ than himself. Thus, it is false that there is somebody who is smarter than anybody.

(Universe: people)

453 From a newspaper column:

> *Retail Credit's little second floor office in North Miami would never lead you to believe that Retail Credit owns the Credit Bureau of Greater Miami, a huge firm which keeps a computerized eye on most Dade Countians from its elaborate headquarters at 14701 NW 7th Avenue.*
>
> *Ownership works out this way: The Credit Bureau of Greater Miami is owned by Credit Bureau, Inc., of Atlanta, a wholly owned subsidiary of Retail Credit Co.[1]*

The conclusion is given in the first paragraph, and two premises are supplied in the second. Add this auxiliary premise: ' "Owning" is a transitive

---

[1] Jack Roberts, "Miamian Wages War on Retail Credit Co.," *Miami News,* February 15, 1973, p. 5-A.

relation'.[2] (r = Retail Credit Co., m = Credit Bureau of Greater Miami, a = Credit Bureau, Inc., of Atlanta, Oxy = x owns y)

454 Sign on the back of a bus:

> *Borden's Ice Cream—*
> *Better Than Anything*

This slogan, taken literally, is false, as the following argument shows:

> Nothing is BETTER$_R$ than itself. So, It is false that Borden's ice cream is better than anything.

455 Logician D. C. Makinson:

> *The relation of subtending is not transitive.[3] For example, p ∧⏋ p subtends (p ∨ q) ∧⏋ p, and the latter subtends q, but as we have already seen, p ∧⏋ p does not subtend q.[4]*

This argument is presented conclusion first. (Universe: formulas; Sxy = x subtends y, a = the formula 'p ∧⏋ p', b = the formula '(p ∨ q) ∧⏋ p', c = the formula 'q')

456 If a PERSON SMOKES$_R$ he ENDANGERS his health—no matter what the substance smoked. It follows that people who smoke "pot" endanger their health.

(Mx = x is "pot")

457 During the final days of the Nixon presidency, a television newscaster raised the question of whether or not a president can pardon himself. He then cited a nineteenth-century Supreme Court decision that the president's power to grant pardons is unlimited, suggesting this argument:

> A PRESIDENT can pardon himself, since he can pardon anyone.

(Universe: people; Cxy = x can pardon y)

---

[2] A transitive relation is one such that if any individual bears the relation to a second and the second bears it to a third, then the first bears it to the third.
[3] See 453.
[4] *Topics in Modern Logic* (London: Methuen & Co. Ltd., 1973), p. 28.

458 In "Irish Sketches," John McCarten tells about a terrier biting his friend Fiach while they were touring in Ireland. The dog's owner comforted Fiach by noting, "Thank God there is no rabies in Ireland, so you don't have to worry about going mad."[5] These words may have provided small comfort, but they summarize valid reasoning.

> One animal will CONTRACT$_R$ rabies from another only if the latter is RABID. This <u>terrier</u> is from IRELAND. Therefore, <u>Fiach</u> will not get rabies from the terrier, because no Irish animals have rabies.

(Universe: animals; $Cxy = x$ contracts rabies from y)

459 The jury supposedly reasoned:

> The <u>client</u> is no MORE$_R$ guilty than the <u>lawyer</u>. And the client is GUILTY. But if A is no more guilty than B, and A is guilty, then B is also guilty. Hence, the lawyer must be guilty.

($Mxy = x$ is more guilty than y, $Gx = x$ is guilty)

"'Your mistake was telling the jury, 'My client is no more guilty than I am!'"

GRIN AND BEAR IT by George Lichty. © Field Enterprises, Inc., 1973. Courtesy of Field Newspaper Syndicate.

[5] *The New Yorker*, November 20, 1971, pp. 195–96.

460   Headline on an advertisement:

> *Since pollution is everybody's fault, everybody is responsible for curbing it.*

Add this suppressed premise, 'If something is somebody's fault, then they are responsible for curbing it'. (p = pollution, $Px = x$ is a person, $Fxy = x$ is the fault of y, $Rxy = x$ is responsible for curbing y)

461   From a newspaper sports story:

> *Dolphins season seats remain in Sections A, M, 11 and 22 on the north and Y, N, 34 and 23 on the south side as well as in the west end zone.*
>
> *They are the best seats available because they are the only seats available.*[6]

The reporter reasoned,

> Every seat DESCRIBED above is BETTER$_R$ than any available seat not described, because the described seats are the only seats available.

(Universe: available seats)

462   The philosopher Peter Caws writes:

> *Taken as an element of a formal system, a sentence can be analytic only if the axioms from which it ultimately derives are analytic. Every proof in a formal system is analytic . . . but the theorem proved is not analytic unless the axioms are.*[7]

Caws has committed a logical error. If the axioms of a consistent formal system are analytic, then the theorems must be analytic also; but it is false that if the *theorems* are analytic, the *axioms* must be analytic. The following miniature formal system is proof of this:

[6] "4,680 New OB Seats Planned by Sept. 10," *Miami News*, August 8, 1972, p. 1-B.
[7] *The Philosophy of Science* (Princeton, N.J.: D. Van Nostrand Co., Inc., 1965), p. 136.

AXIOMS: (A1) If it is snowing, school will be cancelled.
(A2) If school will be cancelled, it is snowing.
THEOREM: (T1) If it is snowing, it is snowing.

Argument 462 drives the criticism home.

T1 is DERIVED$_R$ from the <u>axiom</u> set composed of A1 and A2.
T1 is ANALYTIC, but the axiom set is not. Therefore, the claim
that a theorem is analytic only if the axioms from which it
derives are analytic is false.

($t = $ T1, $Dxy = x$ is a theorem derived from axiom set y, $a = $ the axiom
set composed of A1 and A2)

463 Breakfast-table dialogue:

Mark (age four): "I'm spying at Michael."

Amy (age six): "Spying means looking at somebody and they don't
know you're doing it. Michael knows you're looking at him, so that's
not spying."

Prove Amy's reasoning valid. Her first statement is definitional; symbolize
it as a (universally quantified) biconditional. Use these symbols:

$Sxy = x$ spies on y
$Lxy = x$ looks at y
$Kxy = x$ knows that y is looking at x
    $a = $ Michael
    $b = $ Mark

(Universe: people)

464 TOBACCO companies actually FAVOR$_R$ the WARNINGS that
they are required to print on cigarette packages, because these
warnings REDUCE their liability in damage suits brought
against them by ill ex-smokers, and the warnings accomplish
this without DECREASING the sales of cigarettes. Obviously
the tobacco companies favor anything that reduces liability
without hurting cigarette sales.

($Rx = x$ reduces the liability of tobacco companies in damage suits, Dx
$= x$ decreases cigarette sales)

465 William James's principal argument for indeterminism may be paraphrased as follows: [8]

> <u>Indeterminism</u> SATISFIES$_R$ human needs more adequately than does <u>determinism</u>. Of two conceptions, the one that more adequately satisfies human needs is the more RATIONAL$_R$. Of two conceptions, we are ENTITLED$_R$ to suppose that the more rational is the truer. Thus, we are entitled to suppose indeterminism to be truer than determinism.

(Universe: conceptions; $Sxy = x$ satisfies human needs more adequately than y, $Exy = $ we are entitled to suppose x to be truer than y)

466 Some fundamentalists maintain that every descendent of Adam possesses original sin. In order to escape attributing original sin to Jesus, they appeal to the doctrine of the virgin birth. However, as 466 shows, the virgin-birth theory is not by itself sufficient to remove Jesus from the scope of the fundamentalist claim about original sin. [9]

> Every DESCENDENT$_R$ of <u>Adam</u> possesses ORIGINAL sin. <u>Mary</u> is a descendent of Adam. <u>Jesus</u> is a descendent of Mary. "Descendence" is a transitive relation. [10] Thus, Jesus possessed original sin.

(Universe: people)

467 A skeptical argument:

> A PERSON can KNOW$_R$ something only if it is IMPOSSIBLE$_R$ for him or her to be mistaken about it. [11] Nothing relating to SENSE experience is such that it is impossible for a person to be mistaken about it. Accordingly, no person knows anything that relates to sense experience.

($Ixy = $ it is impossible for x to be mistaken about y, $Sx = x$ relates to sense experience)

---

[8] James argues for the first and third premises in "The Dilemma of Determinism," and for the second premise in "The Sentiment of Rationality," in *Essays in Pragmatism*, ed. Alburey Castell (New York: Hafner Publishing Co., Inc., 1948).

[9] The Catholic doctrine of the immaculate conception of Mary is an attempted resolution of this problem.

[10] See 453.

[11] It is important to distinguish this false claim from the true statement 'A person can know something only if he or she is not mistaken about it'.

468 An attack on the first premise of the preceding argument:

> This statement is false: a PERSON can KNOW$_R$ something only
> if it is IMPOSSIBLE$_R$ for him or her to be mistaken about it.
> Its falsity follows from two facts: (1) only LOGICO-mathematical
> truths are such that it is impossible for a person to be
> mistaken about them; and (2) there are people who know
> something other than logico-mathematical truths.

469 A bumper sticker:

> *BABIES ARE PEOPLE*
> *ABORTION KILLS PEOPLE*

The following argument is advanced:

> Every BABY is a PERSON. Every act of ABORTION RESULTS$_R$
> in the death of a baby.[12] Thus, every act of abortion results in
> the death of a person.

($Rxy = x$ results in the death of y)

470 Logician W. V. Quine writes:

> *The sentence '$\sim(x \in x)$' determines no set. If there were such a
> set, it would have to be a member of itself if and only if not a
> member of itself.*[13]

The first sentence is the argument's conclusion. (Universe: sets; $Dx = x$
is determined by the sentence '$\sim (x \in x)$', $Mxy = x$ is a member of y)

471 A PERSON ADDICTED$_R$ to <u>alcohol</u> is a DRUG addict—because
alcohol is a drug.

($Dx = x$ is a drug)

472 Excerpt from a column by Carl Rowan:

> *K. C. Jones and his Washington Bullets and Al Attles and his*

---

[12] This premise is false; a fetus is not a baby.
[13] *Philosophy of Logic* (Englewood Cliffs, N.J.: Prentice-Hall, Inc., 1970),
p. 45.

Golden State Warriors have already destroyed the racist notion that blacks are heap much muscle, no gray matter. Did it ever dawn on you that the two basketball coaches now strategizing and dueling for the world championship are blacks? [14]

Rowan's argument could be formalized:

The <u>Bullets</u> or the <u>Warriors</u> will be the NBA champions. K. C. <u>Jones</u>, the COACH$_R$ of the Bullets, is BLACK. And Al <u>Attles</u>, the coach of the Warriors, is also black. It follows that some NBA championship team will have a black coach.

($Nx = x$ is an NBA championship team)

473 The doctrine of *representative perception* maintains that our sensations are caused by material objects and that the sensations represent or picture these objects. Berkeley attacked this doctrine with several arguments, including 473.[15]

Our SENSATIONS are not CAUSES. Anything that REPRESENTS$_R$ something that is a cause must itself be a cause. So, it is false that there are sensations that represent things that are causes.

474 Dave's Gas Station advertises that it "specializes in the repair of all American and foreign cars." Argument 474 convicts Dave of misusing the concept "specialize."

No GARAGE SPECIALIZES$_R$ in the repair of *all* CARS [because of the meaning of the word 'specialize']. <u>Dave's</u> Gas Station is a garage. Any car is either AMERICAN or FOREIGN. This shows it is false that Dave's Gas Station specializes in the repair of all American and foreign cars.

($Sxy = x$ specializes in the repair of y)

475 In the preface to his classic study of mythology, Thomas Bulfinch wrote:

---

[14] Carl T. Rowan, "Of Brains and Brawn," *Miami News*, May 27, 1975, p. 11-A. Reprinted by permission.

[15] See *A Treatise Concerning the Principles of Human Knowledge* (Indianapolis, Ind.: The Bobbs-Merrill Co., Inc., 1957), p. 35.

If that which tends to make us happier and better can be called useful, then we claim that epithet for our subject. For mythology is the handmaiden of literature; and literature is one of the best allies of virtue and promoters of happiness.[16]

Bulfinch's reasoning:

Mythology ASSISTS$_R$ literature. Literature PROMOTES$_R$ virtue and happiness. If *A* assists *B* and *B* promotes *C*, then *A* promotes *C*. Therefore, if whatever promotes both happiness and virtue is USEFUL, then mythology is useful.

476 A peculiarity of the theory that laws are the commands of the sovereign is made clear by argument 476.

An individual is LEGALLY$_R$ bound to do something if and only if the sovereign COMMANDS$_R$ him to do it. No individual can command himself to do anything. It follows that the sovereign is not legally bound to do anything.

($Cxyz$ = *x* commands *y* to do *z*)

477 An Associated Press story:

ALAMEDA, Calif.—A Soviet freighter has been seized at this San Francisco Bay port by federal marshals as security for a $377,000 damage suit filed by New England fishermen who claim Russian trawlers destroyed their lobster fishing gear.

Deputy U.S. Marshal Clifford Cline and three other marshals boarded the Suleyman Stalskiy late yesterday. . . .

. . . Cline said, "The Russian government owns all Russian ships so we are seizing this one." Maritime law permits any of a shipowner's vessels to be held as security for a damage claim.[17]

[16] *The Outline of Mythology* (New York: The Review of Reviews Corporation, 1913), p. v.

[17] "Russian Freighter Seized in U.S. Port Over Damage Suit" (Associated Press), *Miami News,* June 10, 1971, p. 8-A.

Marshal Cline's argument:

> Any VESSEL owned by a SHIPOWNER against whom there is a
> damage claim may be HELD as security. The Russian
> government, which OWNS$_R$ all RUSSIAN vessels, is such a
> shipowner. Hence, the <u>Suleyman</u> Stalskiy may be held for
> security, since it is a Russian vessel.

($Sx = x$ is a shipowner against whom there is a damage claim, $Hx = x$
may be held for security)

478 One statement ENTAILS$_R$ a second if and only if it is logically
IMPOSSIBLE$_R$ for the first to be true and the second false.
For any two statements, if the second is LOGICALLY true then
it is logically impossible for the first to be true and the
second false. This proves that a logically true statement is
entailed by every statement.

(Universe: statements; $Ixy =$ it is logically impossible for x to be true
and y false)

479 A story in *Newsweek* concerns Christian sects in Appalachia that
practice snake-handling. Cult members stress Mark 16:16–18.

> *He that believeth and is baptized shall be saved . . . ; they shall*
> *take up serpents; and if they drink any deadly thing, it shall not*
> *hurt them.*

The story notes that practitioners of these reptilian rituals "refuse treatment when bitten; if they die, it is taken as a sign of insufficient faith." [18]
Apparently they "reason" as follows:

> TRUE believers who are BAPTIZED are SAVED. He who is
> saved can be HARMED$_R$ by no POISONOUS snake.
> Consequently, if some poisonous snake harms one who has
> been baptized, the latter is not a true believer.

[18] "Americana: The Lord's Bidding," April 23, 1973, p. 23.

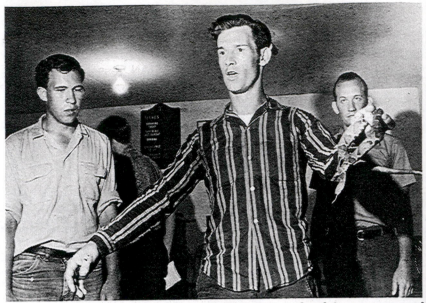

Photograph reproduced by permission of *Knoxville News Sentinel.*

480 In the *Meno,* Plato writes:

> Socrates: *I know, Meno, what you mean. . . . You argue that a man cannot enquire either about that which he knows, or about that which he does not know; for if he knows, he has no need to enquire; and if not, he cannot; for he does not know the very subject about which he is to enquire.*[19]

This reasoning is paraphrased by 480.

> If one already KNOWS$_R$ a proposition, then one cannot COME$_R$ to know it. If, on the other hand, one does not already know a proposition, then one cannot RECOGNIZE$_R$ it as what one desired to know. And if one cannot recognize a proposition as that which he desired to know, then one cannot come to know it. It follows, then, that no one comes to know any proposition.

(Px = x is a person, Kxy = x already knows y, Ax = x is a proposition,

[19] *The Dialogues of Plato,* 2 vols., trans. B. Jowett (New York: Random House, 1892), I, 360.

$Cxy = x$ comes to know y, $Rxy = x$ recognizes y as that which x desired to know)

481 No UNIVERSITY that operates on an inadequate budget should ENGAGE$_R$ in any expensive programs that are not essential either to ACADEMIC excellence or to student WELFARE. Therefore, no university on an inadequate budget should participate in any of the major INTERCOLLEGIATE sports, since all the major intercollegiate sports are costly and none are essential either to academic excellence or to the welfare of students.

($Ux = x$ is a university that operates on an inadequate budget, $Exy = x$ should engage in y, $Mx = x$ is expensive, $Ax = x$ is essential to academic excellence, $Wx = x$ is essential to student welfare)

482 Logicians Hughes and Cresswell write:

> *An axiomatic system is said to be* consistent *iff [if and only if] no thesis is the negation of any other thesis. (Stated without reference to interpretation, the condition is that for no wff [well-formed formula], a, are both a and $\sim a$ theses.)*

> *PM is consistent in this sense. The simplest way of proving this is to show (a) that every axiom is valid; (b) that the transformation rules are validity-preserving; and (c) that if a wff, a, is valid, then $\sim a$ is not valid.*[20]

A simplified version of their argument:

Every THESIS of pm is VALID [since every axiom of pm is valid, and the transformation rules are validity-preserving]. No valid wff of pm has a NEGATION$_R$ that is valid. Hence, no thesis of pm has a negation that is a thesis.

(Universe: wffs of pm; $Nxy = x$ is a negation of y)

---

[20] G. E. Hughes and M. J. Cresswell, *An Introduction to Modal Logic* (London: Methuen and Co. Ltd., 1968), p. 19.

483 The Aristotelian and Ptolemaic theory that the earth is the fixed center of the universe was supported by this argument (among others): [21]

> If one CELESTIAL body REVOLVES$_R$ around some object, then [as there is regularity in the heavens] all the celestial bodies must revolve around that object. The <u>moon</u> is a celestial body that revolves around our <u>earth</u>. Therefore, all celestial bodies revolve around the earth.

484 The main assumption of 483 was brought into question by Galileo's discovery of the satellites of Jupiter.[22]

> There is at least one CELESTIAL body that REVOLVES$_R$ around <u>Jupiter</u>. The <u>moon</u> is a celestial body that does not revolve around Jupiter. So, it is false that if one celestial body revolves around some object, then all the celestial bodies must revolve around that object.

485 Any AMPLIATIVE inference for which there is a COGENT DEDUCTIVE JUSTIFICATION$_R$ is not an ampliative inference. Any nondeductive justification for an ampliative inference is VICIOUSLY circular. Nothing that is viciously circular is cogent. Hence, there is no cogent justification for any ampliative inference.[23]

($Jxy = x$ is a justification for y)

486 A particle of MATTER that is indivisible is not EXTENDED. Anything that lacks extension is nonmaterial. For any DIVISIBLE particle of matter there is a second particle of matter that is SMALLER$_R$ than the first. It follows that there are no smallest particles of matter.[24]

487 If a person knows a statement to be true must he or she also know to be true any statement that is entailed by the first one? The affirmative answer to this question leads to absurd consequences.

---

[21] See Herbert Butterfield, *The Origins of Modern Science* (New York: The Free Press, 1957), pp. 78–79.

[22] Ibid., p. 79.

[23] This is a paraphrase of Wesley Salmon's paraphrase of Hume's argument that induction cannot be justified. See Salmon's *The Foundations of Scientific Inference* (Pittsburgh, Pa.: University of Pittsburgh Press, 1967), p. 11.

[24] Restated: it is not the case that there is something material such that nothing material is smaller than it.

If a PERSON KNOWS$_R$ a STATEMENT to be true, then he or she knows to be true any statement that is ENTAILED$_R$ by the first one. Every person who is not an INFANT knows at least one statement to be true. It follows that every person past infancy knows every LOGICALLY true statement to be true, because [as 478 proved] a logically true statement is entailed by every statement.

($Kxy = x$ knows y to be true, $Exy = x$ entails y)

488   Given any two EXPLANATIONS$_R$ for the same thing, if one is more probable than the other it is preferable to it. For any report of a MIRACULOUS occurrence, there is an explanation for the report that holds it to be FALSE$_R$ and that is more probable than any explanation of the report that does not take the report to be false. Hence, for any miracle report there is an explanation of it that holds the report to be false and that is preferable to any explanation of the report that does not regard it as false.[25]

($Exy = x$ is an explanation for y, $Axy = x$ is more probable than y, $Bxy = x$ is preferable to y, $Mx = x$ is a miracle report, $Fxy = x$ holds y to be false)

489   Consider S1:

(S1)   There is a VILLAGE that has a RESIDENT$_R$ MALE BARBER who SHAVES$_R$ all and only those male residents who do not shave themselves.

S1 is a logical contradiction; it is logically impossible that there be such a village.[26] On first consideration it is not obvious that this *is* a logical impossibility, so it is of interest to prove it. Argument 354 showed that any sentence that entails a contradiction is itself contradictory. Prove that S1 is contradictory by demonstrating that it entails S2, which is obviously contradictory:

(S2)   There is a barber who shaves himself although he does not shave himself.

---

[25] This is adapted freely from Hume, *An Inquiry Concerning Human Understanding* (Indianapolis, Ind.: The Bobbs-Merrill Co., Inc., 1955), section 10.
[26] For a discussion of this and other paradoxes see W. V. Quine, "Paradox," *Scientific American*, CCVI (April 1962), 84–96.

490   In the dialogue *Theatetus,* Plato proves that the square root of a natural number is not a fraction.[27] Argument 490 paraphrases his reasoning.

> The square ROOT$_R$ of a PERFECT square is a NATURAL number. No natural number is a FRACTION. The square root of a natural number other than a perfect square is not a fraction. Therefore, the square root of a natural number is not a fraction.

(Universe: numbers)

491   A DEDUCTIVE system is *complete* if and only if all the TRUE FORMULAS EXPRESSIBLE$_R$ in it are PROVABLE$_R$ as theorems within the system. A deductive system is *consistent* if and only if there is a formula expressible in it that is not provable as a theorem within the system. Therefore, every inconsistent deductive system is complete.

($Ax = x$ is complete, $Pxy = x$ is provable as a theorem in y, $Bx = x$ is consistent)

492   Hobbes writes in the *Leviathan,* "to honor [all] those another honors, is to honor him." [28] Show that this entails that everyone HONORS$_R$ someone. (Universe: people)

493   Philosopher J. N. Findlay argues:

> If an investigation of one topic LEADS$_R$ to a second topic about which CLARITY cannot be attained, then it is impossible to achieve clarity in regard to the first topic. For any PHILOSOPHICAL topic, its investigation will lead to some VALUE topic. So, if there is no clarity to be had in regard to values, there is no clarity to be had on any philosophical topic.[29]

(Universe: topics; $Lxy =$ investigating x leads to y, $Cx =$ clarity can be attained about x)

---

27 See Francis M. Cornford, *Plato's Theory of Knowledge* (Indianapolis, Ind.: The Bobbs-Merrill Co., Inc., 1957), pp. 22–23.
28 (Chicago, Ill.: Henry Regnery Co., 1956), p. 84.
29 See J. N. Findlay, *The Discipline of the Cave* (London: George Allen & Unwin, Ltd., 1966), p. 55.

494 Philosophers of science are anxious to analyze the relationship of *confirmation*—the relationship that exists between two statements when the first constitutes favorable evidence for the second. It has been suggested that one statement confirms a second whenever the second entails the first. It has also been held that if one statement confirms a second, then the first confirms any statement entailed by the second. Nelson Goodman shows that these two claims taken together lead to absurdity.[30]

> One statement CONFIRMS$_R$ a second if and only if the second ENTAILS$_R$ the first. If one statement confirms a second, then the first confirms any statement entailed by the second. Therefore, every statement confirms all statements, because for any two statements, there exists at least one statement that entails both.[31]

(Universe: statements)

495 As the term began, I discovered that the students outnumbered the available texts. Recognizing that some students would likely drop the course, I announced that I would postpone the midterm exam until the number of students had dropped to the number of books. Later I decided I had made a mistake. Argument 495 shows why.

> There will not be ENOUGH books until AFTER$_R$ some students have DROPPED the course. No student will drop out until after the midterm is SCORED. Yet the midterm will not be scored until after it is GIVEN. "Occurring after" is an irreflexive relation.[32] Hence, since the midterm will not be given until after there are enough books, there never will be enough books.

(Universe: moments; Ex = there are enough books at x, Dx = some students drop the course by x, Sx = the midterm is scored at x, Gx = the midterm is given at x)

496 Some logicians introduce a relation between statements that they label "material implication." One statement is said to materially imply

[30] See *Fact, Fiction, and Forecast,* 2nd ed. (Indianapolis, Ind.: The Bobbs-Merrill Co., Inc., 1968), pp. 67–68.
[31] For example, the conjunction of the two statements.
[32] That is, nothing occurs after itself.

a second if and only if the truth-functional conditional that has the first as antecedent and the second as consequent is true. One peculiarity of this relationship is that it is so often exemplified. As 496 shows, the relationship holds (in at least one direction) between any two statements.

> A truth-functional conditional is TRUE if and only if its ANTECEDENT is false or its CONSEQUENT is true. If all truth-functional conditionals with false antecedents are true, then a FALSE statement MATERIALLY$_R$ implies all statements. If all truth-functional conditionals with true consequents are true, then a true statement is materially implied by all statements. Since every statement is either true or false, it follows that for any two statements either the first materially implies the second or the second materially implies the first or each materially implies the other.

(Universe: statements; $Bx = x$ is a truth-functional conditional, $Ax =$ the antecedent of x is false, $Cx =$ the consequent of x is true)

497 If two football teams PLAY$_R$ one another, they will not both win. "Playing one another" is a symmetrical relation.[33] So, if two football teams play each other, at most one of them will win all its games.

(Universe: football teams; $Dxy = x$ defeats y)

498 (CHALLENGE) What is the nature of the inference from observational evidence to the scientific hypothesis that explains the evidence? It can be proved conclusively that the inference is not deductive.[34]

> For any OBSERVATION statement and any HYPOTHESIS, there exists a second hypothesis that is logically COMPATIBLE$_R$ with the observation statement but not with the first hypothesis. "Logical compatibility" is a symmetrical relationship.[35] Any two statements are logically incompatible if and only if there

---

[33] That is, if team A plays team B, then team B plays team A.

[34] This argument is found in Wesley Salmon, *The Foundations of Scientific Inference* (Pittsburgh, Pa.: University of Pittsburgh Press, 1967), p. 19.

[35] That is, if one statement is logically compatible with a second, then the second is logically compatible with the first.

exists a statement that is a DENIAL$_R$ of the second statement and is entailed by the first statement. "Entailment" is transitive.[36] All of this proves that no observation statement ENTAILS$_R$ any hypothesis.

Notice that the second, third, and fourth premises are purely logical; their function is to facilitate the derivation of the conclusion from the first premise. (Universe: statements)

499 (CHALLENGE) Some philosophers employ the concept of "volition" in order to handle certain difficult philosophical problems, notably the freewill problem. The volition theory, however, can easily lead to absurdities, as 499 shows.

Every FREE ACT is caused by a VOLITION. Volitions are acts. No act caused by a nonfree volition is free. Therefore, any volition that CAUSES$_R$ a free act is itself caused by a volition that in turn is caused by a volition.[37]

500 (CHALLENGE) In Book Nine of his *Elements*, Euclid proves that there are an infinite number of primes.[38] His proof is summarized by 500. (Do not symbolize the bracketed material.)

If there exists a GREATEST$_R$ PRIME, then there is a second number [namely, the sum of one and the product of all primes less than or equal to the greatest prime] that is greater than the greatest prime, and if this second number is not a prime, then [since every nonprime has a prime divisor] there exists a third number [a prime divisor of the second number] that is a prime and is greater than the greatest prime. [If this third number were identical to a prime smaller than or equal to the greatest prime, then it would be a divisor of both the second number and the number that is one less than the second

---

[36] See 453.

[37] The "chain" of volitions described in the conclusion may be lengthened indefinitely without destroying the validity of the argument.

[38] *The Thirteen Books of Euclid's Elements,* 3 vols., trans. Sir Thomas L. Heath (New York: Dover Publications, Inc., 1956), proposition 20.

number—which is impossible.] Therefore, there is no greatest prime.

(Universe: numbers; $Gxy = x$ is greater than y)

There's no greater mistake than the hasty conclusion that opinions are worthless because they are badly argued.

T. H. Huxley

4·3 Valid and Invalid Arguments

501 Every number is exceeded by some number. Therefore, there is a number that is GREATER$_R$ than all numbers.

(Universe: numbers)

502 Every number is exceeded by some number. Hence, every number is GREATER$_R$ than some number.

(Universe: numbers)

503 A relation is *intransitive* if and only if for any three (not necessarily distinct) objects if the first bears the relation to the second and the second bears the relation to the third, then the first fails to bear the relation to the third. "Being two inches taller than" is an intransitive relation. The logician E. J. Lemmon says that "being parent of" is an intransitive relation.[39] An undergraduate, Ray Bielec, advanced 503 in order to show that Lemmon is mistaken.

Jocasta was a PARENT$_R$ of Oedipus. Jocasta and Oedipus were

[39] *Beginning Logic* (London: Thomas Nelson and Sons Ltd., 1965), p. 183. The expression 'parent of' is ambiguous; it can denote either a biological relation or a legal relation. Is either relation intransitive? Is the biological relation "father of" intransitive? How about the legal relation?

parents of <u>Polynices</u>. Thus, it is false that "being parent of" is an intransitive relation.[40]

(Universe: people)

504 No one is a BETTER$_R$ quarterback than Kenny <u>Stabler</u>. So, Stabler is a better quarterback than anyone in the NATIONAL conference.

(Universe: people; $Bxy = x$ is a better quarterback than y, $Nx = x$ is in the National Conference)

505 In *The Republic,* Plato writes:

There is something ridiculous in the expression "master of himself"; for the master is also the servant and the servant the master; and in all these modes of speaking the same person is denoted.[41]

Plato may be interpreted as advancing 505.

If A is the MASTER$_R$ of B, then B is the SERVANT$_R$ of A. Therefore, anyone who is master of himself is also servant of himself.

Is this argument valid? (Universe: people)

506 Margaret's argument in the "Dennis the Menace" cartoon on page 148:

It is false that a lighter bird can always fly HIGHER$_R$ than a heavier one. Proof: The <u>buzzard</u> can fly higher than the <u>sparrow</u>. The buzzard weighs MORE$_R$ than the sparrow. "Being able to fly higher than" is an asymmetric relation.[42]

Dennis believes her reasoning to be wrong. Is it? (Universe: bird species)

[40] In other words, it is false that if one person is a parent of a second and the second is a parent of a third, then the first is not a parent of the third.
[41] *The Dialogues of Plato,* 2 vols., trans. B. Jowett (New York: Random House, 1892), I, 694.
[42] A relation, R, is asymmetrical if and only if, if any individual bears R to a second, then the second does not bear R to the first.

"Dennis the Menace" courtesy of Hank Ketcham and copyright Field Newspaper Syndicate TM ®.

507   Descartes writes in *The Principles of Philosophy:*

> *Nothing is possessed of no attributes, properties, or qualities. For this reason, when we perceive any attribute, we therefore conclude that some existing thing or substance to which it may be attributed, is necessarily present.*[43]

The argument restated:

There is nothing that HAS$_R$ no attributes. So, each attribute is possessed by something.

(Hxy = individual x has attribute y)

508   It is not clear whether Irma Thurston means S1 or S2 by 'You always break your shoelace when you're in a hurry'.

(S1)   Every time one breaks his shoelace he is in a hurry.
(S2)   Every time one is in a hurry he breaks his shoelace.

Neither S1 nor S2 is strictly true, but S1 is closer to the truth. If Irma intends S1, her inference may be:

Every time one BREAKS$_R$ his shoelace he is in a HURRY$_R$. This shows that Thirsty has never been in a hurry because he has never broken a shoelace.

(Bxy = x breaks a shoelace at time y, Hxy = x is in a hurry at time y)

© King Features Syndicate, Inc., 1969.

[43] *The Philosophical Works of Descartes*, 2 vols., trans. Elizabeth S. Haldane and G. R. T. Ross (New York: Dover Publications, Inc., 1955), I, 240. See Part I, principle LII.

509 How is the mathematical truth 'There is no largest number' to be symbolized? S1 and S2 are two possible first steps in producing a formula.

(S1) For any x there exists a y such that y is GREATER$_R$ than x.
(S2) It is not the case that there exists an x such that for any y, x is greater than y.

Are S1 and S2 logically equivalent? They are if and only if 509 and 510 are both valid. (In both arguments include this analytic auxiliary premise: ' "Greater than" is an asymmetric relation'.)[44]

S1.   Therefore, S2.

(Universe: numbers)

510 S2.   Therefore, S1.

(Universe: numbers)

511 Since S1 and S2 (see 509) are not logically equivalent, at least one of them must be an incorrect rendering of 'There is no largest number'. We could prove that S2 is a mistaken translation by showing that it follows from a statement that would be true even if there were a largest number. If S2 would be true even if 'There is no largest number' were false, then the two sentences do not say the same thing. If 511 is valid, S2 is a mistaken translation of 'There is no largest number'.

No number is GREATER$_R$ than itself. Thus, S2.

One of the two translations *is* correct. So, if S2 is not correct, S1 is. (Universe: numbers)

512 A philosopher friend of mine hoped to prove that at least one desire of each person ought to be satisfied. His argument consists in disproving the thesis that no desires of anyone should be satisfied. Did he make his case? That is, is 512 valid?

It is false that no DESIRES$_R$ of any PERSON ought to be SATISFIED. So, at least one desire of each person ought to be satisfied.

($Sx = x$ ought to be satisfied)

[44] See 506.

513 A headline in a newspaper advertisement:

> *Don't kid yourself! Your cigarette isn't lowest in "tar" unless it's lower than Carlton.*

The second sentence sounds impressive, but what does it actually mean? For example, does it logically imply that no cigarette has less "tar" than Carlton? Add this analytic auxiliary premise:

> "Having less 'tar' than" is an asymmetric relation.[45]

(Universe: cigarette brands; a = your brand, Lxy = x has less "tar" than y, c = Carlton)

514 An intelligence test administered to first graders included the following item in a section headed, "Judging Logical Validity":

> *All the toys in this box are for children in the first grade. Kathy is in the second grade.*

What can you tell from this story?
(a) There are no toys in the box.
(b) There are no toys in the box for Kathy.
(c) Kathy has her own toys.
(d) Second graders do not like toys.

My son, Michael, chose *b*. Is this answer correct? Evaluate the argument that has as premises the statements in the box plus the analytic premise 'No first graders are second graders', and that has as conclusion answer *b*. (Tx = x is a toy in the box, Axy = x is allowed to play with y, Fx = x is a first grader, k = Kathy, Sx = x is a second grader)

515 Philosopher Carl Hempel writes:

> *Several systems of ethics have claimed the theory of evolution as their basis; but they are in serious conflict with each other even in regard to their most fundamental tenets. . . . It is obvious that these conflicting principles could not have been validly inferred from the theory of evolution—unless indeed that theory were self-contradictory, which does not seem very likely.[46]*

---

[45] See 506.
[46] *Aspects of Scientific Explanation* (New York: The Free Press, 1965), pp. 86–87.

Hempel's reasoning formalized:

> Any two evolutionary ethical systems that are VALIDLY derived from the theory of evolution will not conflict. Consequently, no evolutionary ethical systems are validly derived from the theory of evolution, since every system of evolutionary ethics CONFLICTS$_R$ with some evolutionary ethical system.

(Universe: evolutionary ethical systems; $Vx = x$ is validly derived from the theory of evolution)

516   In 1577, during one of the plagues, Thomas White preached a sermon at Paul's Cross that contained the following remarks:

> *Looke but vppon the common playes of London, and see the multitude that flocketh to them and followeth them: beholde the sumptuous Theater houses, a continuall monument of London prodigalitie and folly. But I vnderstande they are now forbidden bycause of the plague. I like the pollicye well if it hold still, for a disease is but bodged or patched vp that is not cured in the cause, and the cause of plagues is sinne, if you looke to it well: and the cause of sinne are playes: therfore the cause of plagues are playes.*[47]

Granted that this is a joke (we trust), it is still interesting to evaluate the argument.

> Every plague is caused by some SIN, and every play CAUSES$_R$ some sin. "Causation" is a transitive relation.[48] Therefore, every plague is caused by a play.

($Ax = x$ is a plague, $Bx = x$ is a play)

517   Most deductive arguments that have only one premise are either obviously valid or obviously invalid. Argument 517 is an exception.

> Gautama ADMIRED$_R$ all persons who do not admire themselves. So, Gautama admired some self-admirer.

(Universe: people)

---

[47] Quoted in the preface of Hardin Craig's *Shakespeare: The Complete Works* (Glenview, Ill.: Scott, Foresman and Company, 1961), p. 27.
[48] See 453.

518   Biologist E. E. Stanford writes:

> *One of the most comprehensible and one of the most firmly held of biological laws was long ago expressed in the Latin, "Omne vivum ex vivo"—"All life comes from life," or "Life springs only from life."* [49]

Are the two quoted English sentences equivalent? They are if, but only if, both 518 and 519 are valid.

All LIFE COMES$_R$ from life. Hence, life comes only from life.

($Lx = x$ is living, $Cxy = x$ comes from y)

519   LIFE COMES$_R$ only from life. So, all life comes from life.

520   The nineteenth-century logician Augustus De Morgan claimed that traditional logic was unable to evaluate this inference: [50]

HORSES are ANIMALS. Ergo, heads of horses are heads of animals.

($Bxy = x$ is the head of y)

521   Berkeley advances an argument for the existence of God that is based on his philosophical position. [51]

There is a SPIRIT [God] who CAUSES$_R$ all sense ideas, as the following considerations prove: Every sense idea has some cause. Nothing exists except what is either spirit or IDEA. Ideas do not cause anything.

($Ax = x$ is a sense idea)

---

[49] *Man and the Living World,* 2nd ed. (New York: The Macmillan Company, 1951), p. 18.

[50] I. M. Bochenski maintains that De Morgan was wrong—that Aristotle's logic can accommodate exercise 520. See *A History of Formal Logic,* trans. and ed. Ivo Thomas (Notre Dame, Ind.: University of Notre Dame Press, 1961), p. 95.

[51] *A Treatise Concerning the Principles of Human Knowledge* (Indianapolis, Ind.: The Bobbs-Merrill Co., Inc., 1957), pp. 35–38.

522 How are scientific terms ending in 'able', 'uble', 'ible', etc.—so-called "disposition terms"—to be defined? Consider 'soluble' as an example. One suggested definition is

> (D1) A thing is SOLUBLE if and only if it DISSOLVES$_R$ whenever it is put into WATER$_R$.

This definition has been criticized on the grounds that it has the following absurd consequence:

> Everything that is never placed in water is soluble.

Does D1 entail this statement? ($Dxy = x$ dissolves at time y, $Wxy = x$ is placed in water at time y)

523 The philosopher Rudolf Carnap suggests an alternative definition of 'soluble'.[52]

> (D2) If a thing is put into WATER$_R$ at any time, then it is SOLUBLE if and only if it DISSOLVES$_R$ at that time.

Does D2 entail the absurdity that everything that is never placed in water is soluble?

524 Definitions like D2 (see 523) have a characteristic that is unusual for definitions; namely, they have empirical content.[53] The proof of this is that two such sentences taken together can entail an empirical sentence. If a consistent set of sentences entails an empirical sentence, then the set is also empirical. Argument 524 provides an example of this.

> If a thing is close to a SMALL IRON object, then it is MAGNETIC if and only if the iron object moves TOWARD$_R$ it. If a thing moves through a closed wire LOOP$_R$, then it is magnetic if and only if it GENERATES$_R$ an electric current in the loop. From these it follows that anything that is NEAR$_R$ a small iron object and is moving through a closed wire loop

[52] See "Testability and Meaning," in *Readings in the Philosophy of Science*, ed. Herbert Feigl and May Brodbeck (New York: Appleton-Century-Crofts, 1953), p. 53. D2 is called a "partial definition" since it gives a meaning to 'soluble' only in reference to objects placed in water.

[53] This has been noted by the philosopher Carl Hempel in "Fundamentals of Concept Formation in Empirical Science," *International Encyclopedia of Unified Science*, Vol. II, No. 7 (Chicago, Ill.: The University of Chicago Press, 1952), 27–28.

will generate an electric current in the loop if and only if the small iron object moves toward it.

($Lxy = x$ moves through closed wire loop y, $Gxy = x$ generates an electric current in y)

525   A philosopher visiting the University of Miami read a paper containing the following passage:

> *What x did and what x caused are, even grammatically, different sorts of things.*
>
> *They are also different in fact. What I cause is a result of what I do. So if I do y, I do not thereby cause y, since nothing is a result of itself.*

As I understand the passage, he argues:

Each thing I CAUSE$_R$ is a RESULT$_R$ of something I DO$_R$. So, if I do something I do not cause it, since nothing is a result of itself.

($i = $ I, $Rxy = x$ is a result of y, $Dxy = x$ does y)

526   It is frequently claimed that valid deductive reasoning never proceeds from the specific to the general. Is 526 a valid counterexample?

Indira Gandhi is not a EUROPEAN. Therefore, anyone who HATES$_R$ only Europeans does not hate everyone.

(Universe: people)

527   During the Last Supper (according to the account in Matthew [54]), Jesus said to his disciples, "Truly, I say to you, as you did it to one of the least of these my brethren, you did it to me." Somewhat later in his speech he also said, "Truly, I say to you, as you did it not to one of the least of these, you did it not to me." Was the second statement merely a repetition, perhaps for emphasis, of the first statement, or did it introduce a new thought? Rephrased, is 527 valid or invalid?

Anyone who HELPS$_R$ an UNFORTUNATE person helps Jesus.

[54] See Matthew 25:31–46.

Thus, anyone who helps no unfortunate persons does not help Jesus.

(Universe: persons)

528 In any VALID SYLLOGISM, no TERM$_R$ is distributed in the conclusion unless it is also distributed in a premise. Hence, any syllogism whose mood is EOI is invalid, because any syllogism in mood EOI has at least one term that is distributed in a premise but is not distributed in the conclusion.

($Txy = x$ is a term in y, $Cxy = x$ is distributed in the conclusion of y, $Pxy = x$ is distributed in a premise of y, $Ex = x$ is in mood EOI)

529 Philosopher Carl Hempel claims that the following statements are equivalent: [55]

(S1) For any two objects, if they are not both RELATED$_R$ to each other, then the first is related to the second and the second is not related to the first.
(S2) Every object is related to all objects.

Of course, they *are* equivalent if and only if each entails the other.

S1. Thus, S2.

(Universe: objects)

530 **S2. Thus, S1.**

531 A familiar commercial proclaims,

When you're out of Schlitz, you're out of beer!

What is the logical content of this statement? The advertisers would like us to believe that the statement entails 'All [*real*] beer is Schlitz'. Does it? ($Tx = x$ is a time, $Px = x$ is a person, $Hxyz = x$ has y at z, $Sx = x$ is Schlitz, $Bx = x$ is beer)

[55] Carl Hempel, *Aspects of Scientific Explanation* (New York: The Free Press, 1965), p. 14n.

532 The King would probably accept the following argument:

> The moneyless cannot be mugged. This is true because if one individual MUGS$_R$ a second, then there is some money that BELONGS$_R$ to the second and that the first TAKES$_R$ from him.

($Ax = x$ is money, $Txyz = x$ takes y away from z)

THE WIZARD OF ID by permission of Johnny Hart and Field Enterprises, Inc. (December 8, 1971).

533 Proposition XIII of Part I of Spinoza's *Ethics* is 'Substance absolutely infinite is indivisible'. Spinoza's proof for this proposition may be paraphrased: [56]

> If infinite substance is DIVISIBLE, then not all of its PARTS$_R$ are also INFINITE [because no two substances have the same nature]. If infinite substance is divisible, then if none of its parts is infinite, then all of them can CEASE to exist. If infinite substance is divisible and all of its parts can cease to exist, then infinite substance itself can cease to exist. However, infinite substance cannot cease to exist. Therefore, infinite substance is not divisible.

(s = infinite substance, $Cx = x$ can cease to exist)

534 On test day I instructed the class,

> Students will sit so that no student is to the immediate left or immediate right of any student.

[56] See *The Chief Works of Benedict de Spinoza*, 2 vols., trans. R. H. M. Elwes (New York: Dover Publications, Inc., 1951), II, 54.

Could I simply have said the following?

> Students will sit so that no student is to the immediate left of any student.

Yes—assuming argument 534 is valid.

> No student is to the immediate LEFT$_R$ of any student. One student is to the immediate left of a second if and only if the second is to the immediate RIGHT$_R$ of the first. So, no student is to the immediate left or immediate right of any student.

(Universe: students)

535 Does Lincoln's famous aphorism,

> *It is true that you may fool all the people some of the time; you can even fool some of the people all the time; but you can't fool all of the people all the time,*[57]

entail 'There is a person such that some of the time he can be fooled and some of the time he cannot be fooled'? ($Fxy = x$ can be fooled at y, $Px = x$ is a person, $Tx = x$ is a moment of time)

536 (CHALLENGE) A relation is "reflexive" if and only if every object that enters into the relation bears the relation to itself. "Entailment" is such a relation. Two formal descriptions of reflexivity have been suggested.

> (D1) For any two objects, if the first bears R to the second, then the first bears R to itself and the second bears R to itself.
> (D2) For any two objects, if either the first bears R to the second or the second bears R to the first, then the first bears R to itself.

[57] John Bartlett, *Familiar Quotations,* 13th ed. (Boston, Mass.: Little, Brown and Company, 1955), p. 542.

Do these two statements say the same thing, or is one of them weaker than the other? Find out by testing 536 and 537.

> **D1.   Therefore, D2.**

($Rxy = x$ bears R to y)

537 (CHALLENGE)

> **D2.   Therefore, D1.**

538 (CHALLENGE) British Essayist Hilaire Belloc on cats:

> *If it be true that nations have the cats they deserve, then the English people deserve well in cats, for there are none so prosperous or so friendly in all the world.*[58]

Belloc reasons,

> If NATIONS HAVE$_R$ only the CATS they DESERVE$_R$, then England deserves only GOOD cats, for England is a nation that has only good cats.

539 (CHALLENGE) Philosopher Hans Reichenbach writes:

> *It is not always so easy, however, to discover the analytic character of a sentence combination. Consider the combination: "if any two men either love each other or hate each other, then either there is a man who loves all men or for every man there exists some man whom he hates".*[59]

Is the conditional quoted by Reichenbach logically true? Find out by determining whether its antecedent entails its consequent. (Universe: men; $Lxy = x$ loves y, $Hxy = x$ hates y)

540 (CHALLENGE) Leibniz defines "the good man" as "one who loves all men as much as reason allows."[60] Does it follow from this defini-

---

[58] "A Conversation With a Cat," in *A Book of English Essays*, ed. by W. E. Williams (Baltimore, Md.: Penguin Books Inc., 1951), p. 231.

[59] *The Rise of Scientific Philosophy* (Berkeley and Los Angeles, Calif.: University of California Press, 1958), p. 223.

[60] *Leibniz Selections*, ed. Philip P. Wiener (New York: Charles Scribner's Sons, 1951), p. 559.

tion (without the qualification about reason) that there is a person who loves all good persons? That is, is 540 valid?

A person is GOOD if and only if he or she LOVES$_R$ everybody. Hence, there is a person who loves all good people.

(Universe: people)

Logic as an everyday practice, the habit of logical thinking, is too serious a matter to be left to professional logicians: just as politics cannot safely be left to professional politicians.

P. T. Geach

4·4 Natural Arguments

541 "Emory says he is related to Bryan McCall (Tour 3), but not to Sam McCall (Tour 2A). When reminded that Bryan is related to Sam, he said, 'Well, then, so am I.' It takes an outsider to get these folks together on genealogy."

> **T. W. Reynolds,** *High Lands* (by the author, 1964), p. 144.

542 "For any finite length, there is a shorter length. . . . [Thus] there is a length shorter than any finite length."

> **P. T. Geach,** *Logic Matters* (Berkeley and Los Angeles, Calif.: University of California Press, 1972), p. 5. (Geach discusses, but does not advance, this argument.)

543 "DEAR ABBY: Why do basically honest people cheat at bridge? . . ."
    "DEAR FRIENDS: Basically honest people do not cheat at anything. . . ."

> Abigail Van Buren, "Dear Abby" (Chicago Tribune–New York News Syndicate, Inc.), *Miami News*, May 14, 1972, p. 18-A. Reprinted by permission.

544 "There can be no mind-body interaction because brain events can interact only with something located at some place and mental events cannot be located at a place."

> James W. Cornman and Keith Lehrer, *Philosophical Problems and Arguments: An Introduction* (New York: The Macmillan Company, 1968), p. 207. (Cornman and Lehrer examine, but do not advance, this argument.)

545

MOMMA by Mell Lazarus. Courtesy of Mell Lazarus and Field Newspaper Syndicate (November 6, 1975).

546 "To The Editor:

"I wish to protest against the historical errors in a letter to the editor in The Herald of May 25.

"The writer states that the U.S. 'never lost a war, a real war, that is.' On the contrary. The War of 1812 was fought by us as an ally of France against Britain. There is no question that Napoleon lost that war, and we, as his ally, were also defeated. In fact, the British captured our capital city, Washington, and burned the presidential residence.

"Richard A. Hitchcock"

> *Miami Herald*, June 2, 1975, p. 6-A.

547 "A set A is a *subset* of a set B iff [if and only if] there is no member of A that is not a member of B. . . . [Therefore] every set is a subset of itself."

> Geoffrey Hunter, *Metalogic* (Berkeley and Los Angeles, Calif.: University of California Press, 1971), p. 21.

548 "The bigger the burger the better the burger. The burgers are bigger at Burger King."

Jingle from a television commercial

549 (CHALLENGE) "There is an evident absurdity in pretending to demonstrate a matter of fact, or to prove it by any arguments *a priori*. Nothing is demonstrable unless the contrary implies a contradiction. Nothing that is distinctly conceivable implies a contradiction. Whatever we conceive as existent, we can also conceive as nonexistent. There is no being, therefore, whose nonexistence implies a contradiction. Consequently there is no being whose existence is demonstrable. I propose this argument as entirely decisive, and am willing to rest the whole controversy upon it."

David Hume, Dialogues Concerning Na-
tural Religion (New York: Hafner Pub-
lishing Co., Inc., 1951), p. 58.

550 (SUPER CHALLENGE) "It is convenient at this point to explain some of the terminology we shall use in discussing logical systems. . . . If two systems, A and B, have different bases but contain exactly the same theses, we shall say that A and B are *deductively equivalent* or sometimes simply that they are *equivalent*. . . . If every thesis of system A is a thesis of system B (whether or not B contains other theses as well), we shall say that B *contains* A. Thus two systems with distinct bases are deductively equivalent iff each contains the other."

G. E. Hughes and M. J. Cresswell, An In-
troduction to Modal Logic (London: Me-
thuen and Co., Ltd., 1968), pp. 29–30.

Life is not an argument.
Friedrich Nietzsche